GREAT TRADITION
AND
LITTLE TRADITION
IN
THERAVĀDA BUDDHIST
STUDIES

GREAT TRADITION
AND
LITTLE TRADITION
IN
THERAVĀDA BUDDHIST
STUDIES

Terence P. Day

Studies in Asian Thought and Religion
Volume 7

The Edwin Mellen Press
Lewiston/Queenston

Library of Congress Cataloging-in-Publication Data

Day, Terence P., 1930-
    Great tradition and little tradition in Theravāda
Buddhist studies.

        (Studies in Asian thought and religion ; v. 7)
        Bibliography: p.
        Includes index.
        1. Theravāda Buddhism. 2. Sociology, Buddhist--
Asia, Southeastern. 3. Sociology, Buddhist--South
Asia. I. Title. II. Series.
BQ7190.D38   1987   294.3'91   87-15228
ISBN 0-88946-057-4

This is volume 7 in the continuing series
Studies in Asian Thought and Religion
ISBN 0-88946-057-4
Series ISBN 0-88946-050-7

The Edwin Mellen Press   The Edwin Mellen Press
Box 450   Box 67
Lewiston, New York   Queenston, Ontario
USA 14092   L0S 1L0 CANADA

Printed in the United States of America

To Reverend Gerald and Kathleen Westcott of
Harrogate: *Parentes in Christo*

To my wife, Meena and children, Maya, Anita and
Naveen

TABLE OF CONTENTS

GREAT TRADITION
AND
LITTLE TRADITION
IN
THERAVĀDA BUDDHIST
STUDIES

Preface

The time is ripe for a new historiography of Theravāda Buddhism. It would culminate a comprehensive review and revision which had been envisaged in the early nineteen-sixties. It would be a fruition of two decades of sociological research on "traditional religions" in contemporary Buddhist South Asia. It would set the record straight on how the Great Tradition originated and on the succession of its transformations as it spread from mainland India into mainland Southeast Asia. Above all the new "history" would incorporate the crucial sociological distinction between the "normative" and the "historic" Theravāda Buddhism, especially the folk-forms of the historic tradition through which its religion became regionally localized among the Theravāda Buddhist majority-populations of South Asia.

Great Tradition and Little Tradition in Theravāda Buddhist Studies is an examination and discussion of representative researches during the nineteen-sixties and seventies on religions in Buddhist South Asia which have in common the utilization of a paradigm of peasant socio-cultures which had been developed by Robert Redfield and his associates in Chicago University's School of Anthropology, and which they made applicable to the scientific study of "heterogenetic" or hybrid religious systems such as "Sanskritic Hinduism" and Theravāda Buddhism. The sociological researchers who applied the paradigm to the religious complexes of contemporary Buddhist South Asia explored Buddhism's "normative" and "non-normative" forms and thereby raised crucial historical as well as sociological questions in regard to the development of Theravāda Buddhism in South and Southeast Asia.

The resolution of the historical issues, however, waited upon a consensus between sociologists and historians on the "real" character of "historic" Theravāda Buddhism based on conclusions guided by the concepts, principles, and methodologies of the theoretical and empirical study of religions enunciated as the mandate of religionswissenschaft (science of religion) by the International Association for the History of Religions (IAHR) in the mid nineteen-fifties. The realization of such a consensus was prevented by the informational ambiguities stemming from historical and sociological studies having contrasting informational fields and strategic objectives. These conflicting objectives became sharply accentuated during the proceedings of the 1975 IAHR at the peak of the tidal wave of North American sociological studies on Buddhism which overwhelmed a century and more of Buddhological and Indological studies. Buddhology, with its strong penchant for textual studies, seemed pushed into a corner by the new hybrid discipline of "Buddhist Studies" appearing as an academic compromise between "Religion" and "Asian Studies" in North America's older universities.

Although this seemed to Charles Prebish (1983.323-330) as a crisis of identity and direction in contemporary North American studies of Buddhism, the development may also be interpreted as a movement in North American scholarship on Buddhism beyond its inherited European roots and identity toward a distinctive "American-Type" of scholarship transcending the philosophically-oriented, linguistic exegetical approach of the Franco-Belgian Buddhology and the philological exegeses developed in Anglo-German Buddhological scholarship. This new emphasis in North American Buddhological scholarship developed from a sociological approach to Buddhism occurring within

broader sociological explorations of South and Southeast
Asian socio-cultures which had been richly funded
between the late nineteen-forties and the late nineteen-
sixties by the Ford and the Rockefeller Foundations as
well as by the United States' "Fullbright program." An
harmonization with the older textual-historical approach
to Buddhism began to be adumbrated, before the end of
the nineteen-seventies in terms of the "socio-history"
of Buddhism in Buddhological and sociological studies by
Heinz Bechert and Stanley J. Tambiah.

The present study of their works and the works of
their associates and contemporaries was generously
helped through research funding by the Social Sciences
and Humanities Research Council of the University of
Manitoba. Its publication was facilitated by a
subvention from the Canadian Federation for the
Humanities using funds provided by the Social Sciences
and Humanities Research Council. The Federation's
scholarly evaluators not only recognized and supported
its publication as a distinctive contribution to
scholarship in Religion studies, but also provided the
insightful critique and practical advice which
substantially improved its subsequent revisions.

Canadian studies on Buddhism have received a recent
fillip from The Edwin Mellen Press through its program
on Studies in Asian Thought and Religion. This work is
Volume 7 in its series. The quality of the graphics in
Chapter Five owes much to the skill and experience of my
friend and colleague in the University of Manitoba, Dr.
Ramesh Tiwari particularly the concluding "biospherical
representation" of Southeast Asian Theravada Buddhism in
that chapter which best reflects his practical
encouragement of my interest in the socio-history of
Theravāda Buddhism. My last acknowledged debt is the

community of gifted and dedicated scholars whose field researches and insightful interpretations of the religions of Buddhist South Asia informed and guided this author's efforts in representing their findings on the character and historic development of Theravāda Buddhism in South and Southeast Asia.

Terence P. Day

Spring, 1987

Introduction: The History of Theravāda Buddism in the Sociology of Religion

There are substantial and obvious differences between the Theravāda Buddhism of the Pali scriptural canon which is espoused by Buddhist monks, scholars, and intellectuals in Buddhist South Asia and the Buddhist religion of the vast majority of South Asia's Theravāda Buddhists. These differences have provided the central problem dividing academic-historians from socio-anthropologists working in the same empirical field of Buddhism in South Asia. The differences are behind the crucial sociological issue of how the religion of South Asia's Theravāda Buddhists ought to be interpreted and explained without contradicting the older, more prestigious school of Buddhist textual-historical scholarship and its perpetuated conceptions of "normative" Theravāda Buddhism.

The differences have been highlighted by the respective scholarly "approaches" of the historical and the sociological disciplines, and their resolution was eventually sought through a sociological recognition of the essential "historical factor" behind the contemporary forms of Buddhist South Asia's "traditional" religions, and through recognition by historians of the determining influences of the socio-cultural background of Theravāda Buddhism upon its character and transformations in South and Southeast Asia. Within the socio-anthropological study of Buddhist South Asian religions, the reconciliation of the differences became a promising possibility through the eclectic <u>socio-historical perspective</u> which S.J. Tambiah in particular outlined and discussed toward the end of the nineteen-seventies and indicated as a methodological transcendence of the older, still current yet rather abstract, "academic-historical approach" and the far more recent, yet unhistorical, "structural-functional approach" to religions in Buddhist South Asia.

The leading representatives of the socio-anthropology of religions in Buddhist South Asia during the nineteen-sixties and seventies, whose works have been selected for their bearings upon a modern understanding of Theravāda Buddhism and its history include: Michael Ames, Heinz Bechert, John Brohm, Hans-Dieter Evers, A. Thomas Kirsch, Ganganath Obeyesekere, Melford E. Spiro, Stanley J. Tambiah and B.J. Terwiel. Their sociological studies of religion in Buddhist South Asia are specifically notable on account of applying to the Buddhist religion and socio-culture a paradigm of peasant socio-cultures which Robert Redfield developed, with his associates, in the Chicago School of Anthropology during the late nineteen-fifties. Although Redfield, McKim Marriott, Milton Singer, and M.N. Srinivas interpretively utilized the paradigm's concepts and theory of the "Great Tradition" and the "Little Tradition" interrelationships on the hybrid socio-cultures of Latin America and Hindu-India, they also anticipated its interpretational viability for the hybrid or "secondary" Buddhist socio-culture of South Asia. The justification for this Buddhist-world application of the paradigm became amply demonstrated in the researches of social scientists who explored Theravāda Buddhism's socio-cultural background and history.

Their paradigmatic researches are significant also in regard to the "Science of Religion" itself. For they constitute a specific illustration of the phenomena of "paradigm shift" and "paradigm change" which Thomas S. Kuhn perceived as criteria of scientific revolutions.

The published studies by the representative social scientists in the field show the interpretational and the methodological "shifts" of meaning and application of the paradigm comprising a movement from the typical "structural-functionalistic approach" to religions in Buddhist South Asia characteristic of earlier sociological researches during the nineteen-sixties toward an emergent "socio-historical approach" before the close of the nineteen-seventies.

Those "shifts", however, did not lead to a sociological consensus on the character and development of Theravāda Buddhism in South and Southeast Asia. This was prevented primarily by methodological and interpretational problems implicit in the Redfield-Marriott Great Tradition/Little Tradition dichotomy and arising from its applications to religions in Buddhist South Asia. There were also difficulties stemming from sociological acquiescences to the classical definition of Theravāda Buddhism perpetuated by the older and more prestigious "textual-historical school" of modern Buddhist scholarship. This acquiescence not only demarcated the "normative" Theravāda Buddhism from the non-normative "religion of South Asia's Theravāda Buddhists", but also predetermined a partisan sociological attitude whereby the "Theravāda" label was deleted or withheld from every non-normative expression of the religion of South Asia's lay majority of Theravāda Buddhists and was reserved solely for a conceptually-defined normative religion drawn out of the Pali Buddhist canon of scripture.

On the other hand, the search for such a consensus could only have seemed of secondary importance so long as the sociologists perceived their primary research concerns within the field of rural-peasant socio-culture or the aboriginal "little tradition" of the peasant-folk such that any apparent connections with the "Great Tradition" of Theravāda Buddhism could be set aside as accidental, extraneous, or non-essential. But, when the demands of their discipline for a comprehensive review of the religious metasystems of Buddhist South Asia widened the parameters of their sociological inquiries, they became bound to incorporate both the elite and the popular and the peasant forms into their scientific interpretations and explanations of the religions of South Asia's Theravāda Buddhists. Moreover, the "Great Tradition/Little Tradition" socio-cultural paradigm which Robert Redfield and his associates in the Chicago School of Anthropology developed during the late nineteen-fifties proved eminently viable on account both of its conceptual and theoretical framework and its interpretational adaptivity to the specific forms of those traditional religions in Buddhist South Asia.

The character and range of the contributions to scientific knowledge of religions which those applications affected became the sizeable output of a distinctive socio-scientific community. The members are justifiably recognized as belonging to the scientific community inasmuch as they were scores of individual scholars who were cooperatively organized within the same discipline of socio-anthropology and the same scientific enterprise around a common corpus of empirical data on religions in contemporary Buddhist South Asia, who adopted and utilized the same scientific paradigm of the Chicago School, and dialogically exchanged their interpretations in the same journals and platforms of scholarly interchange.

Although a register of this "scientific community" is not presently available, a short list of its members could be drawn out of B.J. Terwiel's bibliographical listing in his preface to a study of Buddhism in Thailand. A. Thomas Kirsch (1977) adopted the list, provided supplementary bibliographical references, and distinguished within the collective body of those scientists their two principal "groups" of the "structural-functionalists" and the followers of "the historical approach." Both Terwiel's and Kirsch's lists, accordingly, are informationally useful particularly since they indicate the methodological -diversification which Redfield's peasant socio-cultural paradigm generated within the socio-anthropology of religions in Buddhist South Asia during the nineteen-sixties and seventies. These diversifications also indicate the transitions in the scientific interpretation and explanation of traditional Buddhism in contemporary South and Southeast Asia which occurred throughout the two decades when the earlier structuralistic "Great Tradition/Little Tradition" dualization of the religions became displaced and transcended by the organically-integrated socio-historical paradigm intimated by S.J. Tambiah toward the end of the nineteen-seventies.

During those decades, this community of social scientists also systematically characterized the componentially-complex structures of the "traditional" religions in Buddhist South Asia which, in turn, exposed to view the intrinsic structural and functional interrelations of their Theravāda and non-Theravāda, Buddhist and non-Buddhist, "sacred" and "profane", and elitist and popular forms, dimensions, and expressions. These distinctions, moreover, raised crucial analytical and historical questions about the "completeness" or the "incompleteness" of Theravāda Buddhism and its need and acceptance of functionally-complementary componential supplementations from regionally-proximate and contemporaneous Buddhist and non-Buddhist "traditional religion" systems.

Since the scientists also represented these structural organizations by imaginative geometrical and organic and diagramatically-visualized forms, the temporal sequence of these representations brings to light the progress of scientific inquiry into the religions during the two-decade period from the earlier static and ahistorical architectonic configurations toward wholistic and organic representations, and from the earlier analytical and structuralistic emphases to the later historical perspective overcoming crucial interpretational problems in the study of "traditional" systems in contemporary South Asia socio-cultures. The goal of these methodological or representational transitions was a scientific understanding of the sequences of structural transformations through which Theravāda Buddhism temporally passed along the corridors of its spatial expansion in South and Southeast Asia from its first to its present centuries.

Chapter One. Great Tradition and Little Tradition in Sociology of Religions

The concepts and theory of peasant socio-cultures which Robert Redfield and his associates in the Chicago School of Anthropology developed during the nineteen-fifties became the distinctive feature of the socio-anthropological studies of religions in Buddhist South Asia. Through expositions of the cultural components of the religions in terms of the functional, interrelational, and developmental dynamics of a "Great Tradition" and "Little Tradition" the social scientists brought to light new insights on the real character and probably development of Theravāda Buddhism in South and Southeast Asia.

Robert Redfield pioneered their "socio-historical approach" by adapting the current civilizational concepts of "Great Tradition" and "Little Tradition" into an interpretational methodology for the social sciences. In The Little Community (1953) and Peasant Society and Culture (1956), Redfield laid foundations for the scientific application of the concepts to the sociological definition of "society," "culture," and "civilization" in the context of presently surviving "secondary civilizations," their socio-cultures, and their integrated "village-city-town" spatial and temporal networks. Moreover, although the "secondary civilizations" of Latin America and mainland India provided his primary illustrations of the concepts and theory, he perceived these to be appropriate also for socio-anthropological explanations of the hybrid socio-cultural systems of "Buddhist" South and Southeast Asia. In this regard, Redfield indicated the agenda for the new socio-anthropological study of traditional Buddhism in contemporary Buddhist South Asia.

McKim Marriott followed up on Redfield's leads in

an essay on "Little Communities in an Indigenous Civilization" (1955) where his interpretation of the socio-culture of a typical North Indian village was presented as a specific illustration of Redfield's "Great Tradition/Little Tradition" dichotomy by showing a "little tradition" folk-religion infused by the "Great Tradition" of "Sanskritic Hinduism."

Milton Singer, the third leading member of the Chicago team, applied Redfield's concepts and theory to urban popular Hinduism, specifically as found in the modern metropolitan city of Madras and its environs, and especially in terms of the dynamic influences of western-type modernity and modernization bringing a Western "Great Tradition" to bear upon Madras's hybrid ("Great Tradition/Little Tradition") complex of Sanskritic-Hinduism.

A. Redfield's Interpretation of Great Tradition and Little Tradition Interaction in Peasant Socio-Cultures

Redfield adapted the current civilizational concepts of the "Great" and the "Little" Traditions to his "sociology" of "traditional" and "modern" religions which he represented as socio-cultural systems having an historical background of civilizational development.[1] Redfield (1955:43) assumed that: "In a civilization there is a great tradition of the reflective few, and there is a little tradition of the largely unreflective many." The one is "cultivated in schools and temples," and the other "works itself out and keeps itself going in the lives of the unlettered in their village communities." In effect, the "great tradition" is actively disseminated and perpetuated while the "little tradition" more passively perpetuates itself.

Redfield understood, however, that neither of the two traditions ever existed independently, but developed integrally with each other. The two traditions "have long affected each other and continue to do so." The higher tradition in any socio-culture arises partly as a sophistication of its peasant-folk traditions, and an indigenization of that higher tradition through its appropriation by the peasant-folk "in ways not intended by [its] teachers." The "great" and the "little" traditions, therefore, are perceptible as "two currents of thought and action, distinguishable, yet ever flowing into and out of each other," or otherwise, as parallel concurrent developments representable by the diverging and converging lines of "those histomaps or diagrams we sometimes see, showing the rise and change through time of religions and civilizations."

Redfield (1955:44) illustrated his argument from "typical" societies showing that the interdependence of the traditions - like the physical interrelations of a society's elites and laity - is least close in societies which do not represent "the great world civilizations." Moreover, most "non-European societies" could be serially listed according to the degree to which "a distinguishable great tradition" is present, or by the greater or lesser proximity of its "hierarchic" and "lay" traditions.

Redfield also distinguished "primary" and "secondary" civilizations. The former are found in India and China where "the civilization is indigenous, having developed out of the precivilized peoples of that very culture." The latter are found in the peasant societies of Latin America "whose record of events is overlaid with the strong impress of another civilization that invaded America from abroad". This distinction proved useful also for the sociological explanation of South and Southeast Asian Buddhism where an aboriginal and indigenous civilization and socio-culture belonging

to each of its national regions appeared to be strongly
overlaid by the Hindu and Buddhist civilizations
introduced into South and Southeast Asia from mainland
India. Moreover, the civilization and socio-culture of
Buddhist South Asia perceptibly displayed the typical
acculturative and assimilative processes behind the
formation of any "secondary civilization" where a "great
tradition" has supplanted - though never completely - a
"native great tradition" without the "decapitation" or
"deculturation" or replacement or "removal" which A.V.
Kidder observed to have been the fate of South America's
aboriginal "great tradition" following the Spanish
conquest.

A crucial supposition behind Redfield's
presentation was that his definitional distinctions
comprise only a tentative conceptual framework for an
anthropological interpretation of primary civilizations
emerging by way of an hypothetical "little tradition" of
the peasant-folk and through "the interaction of peasant
and philosopher representatives of local culture and
makers of that civilization." But in his interpretative
scheme the "little tradition" is an anthropologists's
conceptual starting-point. As Redfield (1955:46)
explained, the anthropologist "enters his research on
civilization by the back door" of contemporary village-
cultures whose explanation, however, necessitates
references to the civilizational interactions of its
historic past.

In this regard, Redfield assumed that an historical
perspective is essential for a scientific "anthropology"
of civilizations, cultures, and religions which clearly
show the historical bearings of a culture's art,
literature, and religion, etc. upon the meaning of
contemporary anthropological data. Redfield did not
apparently recognize that there might be a reciprocal

interpretation of contemporary forms of a tradition which could complement and correctively balance the arms-length approach of historians to ancient traditions principally by drawing attention to historical factors behind their contemporary forms and manifestations. Redfield's concepts and theory of folk-cultures nevertheless indicated the mechanisms and processes of cultural/historical evolution, particularly through the diffraction and diffusion of ideas by which the burgeoning forms of a hybrid "secondary civilization" and its socio-cultures became historically actualized. The fusion of anthropological and historical perspectives could have forestalled one-sided emphases such as a recognition of historically distinctive "levels" of religious belief and practice in Buddhist South Asia - "the level of the masses and the level of the enlightened" - attributing historical significance solely to the latter.[2] Instead, all the "levels" could be historically interpreted in Redfieldian terms of developmental Great Tradition/Little Tradition cultural interchange and specifically in terms of the "Great Tradition/Little Tradition" interrelationship in the religions of Buddhist South Asia.

Redfield (1963:50) understood that anthropologists must not ignore the historical background of their field-data, particularly in respect of the interconnection of contemporary popular religious belief and practice with the "philosophy and refined schools of thought" and its present professional representatives, or the "traces" within it of the higher tradition which has survived in the villages.[3] Elsewhere, Redfield (1955:50) explained that the anthropologist who has "taken on responsibility for the study of a composite socio-cultural structure composed of great and little traditions which have interacted from the past to the

present day" necessarily shares that responsibility with
the historian and the humanist. This is because the
distinctive researches of "the humanist-historian" and
the anthropologist are complementary. The historian's
interest is primarily "textual" and focussed on "the
hierarchic culture"; but the anthropologist's interest
is "contextual" in regard to "the context of daily life
as the anthropologist sees it happen." But, the latter
perceives it as the most recent expression of an
historic impingement of "some element of the [textually
transcribed] great tradition" upon the faith and life of
the ordinary people.

    This anthropo-historical complementarity indicates
the feasibility of a reformulated history of a culture
in which the progress of a religion's development is
presented in a socio-historical format as the unfolding
expression and sophistication of the religious component
of people's socio-culture. Redfield even anticipated
such a scientific history. The subsequent socio-
historical studies of Hinduism and Buddhism show the
profound influence of his ideas upon the "academic
historical study" of Hinduism and Buddhism even to the
extent that the textual traditions of the two religions
could be recognized as component cultural artifacts
expressing the socio-cultural complexes within which
those religions historically unfolded. Redfield also
foresaw that the anthropologist's inquiry into the
sophisticated and the folk expressions of socio-cultures
in Hindu and Buddhist South Asia could initiate a
comprehensive revision and review of the current
historiographical record on Hinduism and Buddhism in the
light of socio-anthropological data and could
historically validate the textual-historian's knowledge
of their character and historic development.

The published socio-anthropological researches on Buddhist South Asia during the nineteen-sixties and seventies clearly show the gradual clarification of Redfield's socio-historical intimations. The adumbrations of the structural-historicism are also retraceable from Redfield through Marriott and Singer via Dumont and Pocock on to Tambiah and Heinz Bechert. But it cannot be said that the social scientists who applied Redfieldian concepts to the religions of Buddhist South Asia always carefully heeded Redfield's cautionings about the conceptual and nonhistorical character of the "Great Tradition" and the "Little Tradition" categories used by anthropologists to represent the componential dualities and functional polarities of South and Southeast Asian socio-cultures. Unfortunately, too many social scientists assumed the real and separate existence of two distinctive "traditions" and also their symbiotic rather than their syncretic interrelation throughout the South Asian Buddhist centuries. Redfield (1955:50) instead had precluded a separatistic developmental interpretation by drawing attention to the dimensional commensurality of the two traditions: "because . . . the great tradition is an outgrowth of the little tradition and is now an exemplar for the people who carry the little tradition" . . . "the great and little traditions are dimensions of one another" and are "layers" of the one tradition which the professionals and the laity mutually recognize.[4]

Redfield's observation also precluded suppositions about which of the features and elements of a complex common tradition of the laity and the professionals belong solely to the "great" or the "little" tradition. He admitted that certain features and elements of the tradition belong primarily to the society's professional elites while others are found predominantly in the beliefs, practices, and social systems of the masses. Moreover, it is this selective predilection of the elites and the masses which has supported the misleading notion of two Hinduisms or two Buddhisms, the one of the society's monastic or clerical or intellectual leaderships and the other of the unlettered masses.

B. Marriott on the Mechanisms of "Tradition" Interaction in "Little Community" Cultures

The problem of determining which features and elements of a complex metasystem belong principally to its "Great Tradition" or to its "Little Tradition" dominated Marriott's study of the relation of "hierarchic Hinduism" to Indian-village culture.[5] Marriott used the phrase "hierarchic Hinduism" to connote the Sanskritic "high tradition" or the tradition which is transcribed in Sanskrit sacred texts. He also contrasted this with the "little tradition" in Indian-village Hindu culture which is not textually circumscribed but comprises "the residuum of ideas, beliefs, and practices which have not been brought into the great tradition of India through sanskritization or other acculturative processes." In contrast to Redfield's emphasis on the cultural homogeneity in the "little communities" of India, Marriott recognized instead a dualized complexity which has the "Great Tradition" of Brahmanism as its principal component, and a residual "little tradition" composed of locally-originated ideas, beliefs, and practices.[6] He believed that this duality is apparent in the socio-culture of a Kishan Garhi, a North Indian Hindu village which is typical for the whole of Hindu India.

Marriott also adopted and interpretively applied to its socio-culture in general and to its religious tradition in particular Redfield's concepts of primary and secondary civilizations. He contrasted the "primary civilization", which is an indigenous system which shows historic continuity, with the "secondary civilization" which shows historic discontinuity since it has evolved by the invasion of a "new type of civilization" from abroad.[7] He recognized in the socio-culture of the typical Hindu village of India the primary civilizational type and development. Its folk culture has evolved through an "orthogenetic process" of "straight line . . . indigenous development" by which an aboriginal "Great Tradition" has emerged by "carrying forward . . . cultural materials, norms, and values" hitherto shared by any number of locally-distinctive village-Indian "little traditions."[8]

Marriott's cultural-historical theory of the orthogenetic process of Great Tradition evolution through a synthesis of discrete "little tradition" elements has obvious bearings upon the development of religions in Buddhist South Asia. It implies that an indigenous "Great Tradition" must have existed in South and Southeast Asia centuries prior to any impingement upon it of a Buddhist "Great Tradition" introduced from abroad. In other words, the history of Buddhism in South and Southeast Asia is not in terms of the superimposition of an alien Buddhist "Great Tradition" upon an aboriginal "little tradition" but is instead-in terms of Marriott's "secondary civilization" model-a composite "Great Tradition/Little Tradition" Buddhism merging with the composite orthogenetic "Great Tradition/Little Tradition" of pre-Buddhist South and Southeast Asia.

Marriott's distinctive contribution to modern knowledge on an historic tradition's development is in regard to the dynamic mechanisms through which an indigenous "Great Tradition" generates itself by integrating, cultivating, and universalizing "little tradition" elements. He showed how the process occurs within a network of institutional and functional interlinkages connecting the socio-cultures of individual Hindu villages with the pan-Indian socio-culture. In this regard, "Sanskritic Hinduism" is the resultant historic collectivity of many local and regional socio-cultural complexes of Hindu villages. In this light, the pan-Buddhism of Buddhist South Asia is historically interpretable both as a heterogenetic process whereby an alien-imported tradition became superimposed upon a multitude of aboriginal and non-Buddhist "little traditions", while the regional Buddhism comprises the orthogenetic collectivization of Buddhaized "little tradition" elements.

Marriott explicitly "pursued the implications" of his concept of "indigenous primary civilization" in the socio-cultural laboratory of "one little community"- Kishan Garhi - from two aspects of its socio-cultural data: (i) the relation of the village to "the outside" - specifically to the State and to "the extensive system of castes"; and (ii) the componential complexity of its religion.   Marriott (1955:191) concluded in regard to the first aspect that all the village-communities of present-day India may be conceptualized as "relative structural nexuses" comprising "subsystems within greater systems" or as local, individual identities existing within "a greater field." In this light, the village-communities do not appear as "isolates" existing completely and entirely outside of or under the umbrella of a greater community of India, but as members within the vast network of visible and invisible relations which interconnect the "hundreds of thousands of little communities." He added that it is this socio-cultural network and infrastructure interrelating the multitude of little communities and their "local cultures" throughout Hindu India which is the all-India "Great Tradition" of "Sanskritic Hinduism." The interrelation itself, furthermore, carries crucial implications in regard to "some cultural contents" in the religion of the people of Kishan Garhi specifically in terms of their connection with this "Sanskritic Hindu Great Tradition" civilization.

Marriott (1955:191f.) also considered: (i) the extent to which the religion of a little community can be perceived as an integral whole apart from the religious great tradition in Indian civilization; and (ii) "the extent to which the religious great tradition of Indian civilization is understandable through study of the religion of one little community." He approached these considerations first of all by amplifying the concept of "indigenous primary civilization" into the form of an hypothesis of civilizational development following similar lines to those worked out by Redfield and Singer in "The Cultural Role of Cities" (1954), and by M.N. Srinivas in Religion and Society among the Coorgs of South India (1952). He reductionalistically described "the Great Tradition of Hinduism" as "the literate religious tradition, embodied in, or derived from, Sanskrit works which have a universal spread throughout all parts of India." On the other hand, he recognized its universalized cultural expression in the broad commonality of religious festivals in all the villages which are sanctioned by Sanskrit texts, principally the Rāmāyana and the Purānas. These scripturally-sanctioned festivals show that the Sanskritic-Hindu "Great Tradition" is not peripheral for the religion of the villagers but is integral for it. The "Great Tradition" provides its "Sanskritic rationale and nomenclature" and authorizes its ritualistic transcendences of "the routine barriers of social structure" comprised by caste, lineage grouping, and family.[9]

Marriott (1955:197) also considered how this "Great Tradition" could have contributed to the village culture through many centuries without the peasant-folk religion becoming overwhelmed, absorbed, displaced, or replaced by it. He found an answer in Redfield's and Singer's concept of "universalization." In "The Cultural Role of Cities" (1954:68), he explained that any Great Tradition originates in the primary phase of the evolution of an indigenous civilization by universalizing or generally authorizing "materials already present in the little tradition which it encompasses." This "indigenous" Great Tradition "authorizes" the aboriginal "little tradition" of the villages "when it provides a substantially more articulate and refined restatement or systematization of what is already there." Nevertheless, the Great Tradition "lacks the power for totally supplanting the hoary prototypes that are the sources of its own sacredness" for these are too deeply rooted in the "little tradition." Even their "essentially unlearned and nonliterate nature" obstructs an unimpeded "downward devolution" of Great Tradition elements but allows their pervasive involution and transmutation through "a process of localization [and] . . . reduction to less systematic and less reflective dimensions."[10]

Marriott called this process "parochialization" and indicated its primary illustrations as the popular religious festivals of the Hindu villagers and the pantheon of greater and lesser deities belonging to the village-religion of people such as those of Kishan Garhi. The pantheon is manifestly an integrated system. But, its development has occurred independently of the pantheon of the religious "Great Tradition" of

Sanskritic Hinduism. But, it also comprises elements of the "Great Tradition" pantheon inasmuch as thirty of its ninety deities are universally recognized deities of the "great pantheon." On the other hand, it is not totally commensurate with the higher tradition since "about sixty deities, or two-thirds of the listed total," do not "seem to require us to take much notice of the great tradition of Hinduism." These "little traditional deities" accordingly, together with their respective festivals, rituals, and kinship organizations," represent "an area in which the little community . . . can be conceived as a partly distinctive and partly isolable nexus within greater communities."

S.J. Tambiah and others found Marriott's sophisticated presentation of the "civilizational processes" represented by the concepts of "universalization" and "parochialization" useful for interpreting Buddhism in rural Buddhist South Asia also, particularly in regard to the relationship of the Theravāda Buddhist "Great Tradition" to the aboriginal "little tradition" of the Theravāda Buddhist peasant-folk of South and Southeast Asia. Marriott's concepts and theory are also historically applicable to Theravāda Buddhism in the rural setting of village-Buddhism. For they explain Theravāda Buddhism's efflorations within, not apart from, the indigenous and aboriginal religions of the peasant-folk. Marriott's theory of orthogenetic and heterogenetic civilizational processes indicate also the integrating mechanisms whereby the "Great Tradition" of Theravāda Buddhism could become "parochialized" in and through the pre-Buddhist aboriginal religions, and the latter conversely absorbed into, and thereby "authorized," that is, "buddhaized."

Yet Marriott's ideas on the civilizational mechanisms were not generally accepted. Social

scientists interested in the religions of Buddhist South
Asia found difficulties corresponding to critiques of
Marriott's hypotheses by Dumont and Pocock and by
Stanley J. Tambiah in his preface to a study of Buddhist
and Supernaturalistic Religion in Thailand. Whereas
Dumont and Pocock questioned the analytical utility of
Marriott's idea of "two levels" in Indian culture, the
upper-level of the "hierarchic Sanskritic tradition" and
the lower-level of "popular religion", Tambiah followed
up their critique in six pages of Buddhism and the
Spirit Cults of North-east Thailand (1970:367-373) by
interpreting Marriott's dichotomy and other versions of
it as reflections of the central "cultural-historical
problem" in Indian Sociology which is "how India's past
. . . relates to the present." In the Sociology of
Buddhist South Asia, this translates into the problem of
the nature and the relationship of the various
components and societal "levels" of the religion of
South and Southeast Asia's Theravada Buddhist majority,
specifically how "pre-Buddhist" religion, non-Buddhist
religious elements, and Buddhist components
historically became combined.

Marriott had approached the problem of these
componential interrelations in socio-historical terms of
the "civilizational processes" of "sanskritization" and
"parochialization" which forged the interrelational
nexus of "little tradition" and "great tradition"
religion throughout India's centuries. Dumont and
Pocock had rejected Marriott's hypothesis on the ground
that his dualistic representation of village Hinduism
misrepresented the typical Hindu village as "a real unit
of social life" and its religion by confusing
"disembodied elements of [the] religion" with "the
structure of the religious system itself." [11]

There are grounds for questioning their understanding of Marriott's structural hypothesis on Hinduism in village-India. Nevertheless, their rejection of Marriott's demarkation of the relationship of the Great Tradition and Little Tradition "levels" in India's socio-culture raised the problem of how the complexity of that socio-culture might otherwise be scientifically explained. They rejected Marriott's tradition-dualization of the village religion on the grounds that the villagers of Hindu India have only <u>one</u> "tradition". This is their "village tradition" which "is not conceptually separable into different elements." They rejected Marriott's categorization of the village-tradition as a peripheral "residuum" of the Great Tradition on the grounds that it is not the residue of deities and their festivals found in any one village but not in surrounding villages "but is the whole cycle of festivals studies in their social context." Yet, they provided no satisfactory alternative monolithic theory of the village tradition in Hindu India which could be utilized for a comparable theory of the village tradition in <u>Buddhist</u> South Asia also.

Tambiah, on the other hand, thought that their "several <u>ad hoc</u> assertions" against Marriott's position could be referred also to the Buddhism of rural Buddhist South Asia. Tambiah (1970:369) particularly recognized (i) their supposition (1957:9.15) - that "the lower or popular level of civilization has not only to be recognized but [<u>has also</u>] to be taken as being in some way homogeneous with the higher one" since there is manifestly "some degree of homogeneity between what we know from direct observation and from the literature";[12] (ii) their viewpoint (1957:45) - that "Sanskritization" does not imply the imposition of a <u>different</u> system upon an <u>old</u> one, but the "acceptance of a more distinguished or prestigious way of saying the same thing"; and (iii) their opinion that "the set of relations of 'structures' discovered in the present [village socio-culture] can be fruitfully applied to the understanding of past evidence." Tambiah though, in particular, that this third and historical perception indicates that "one of the contributions an anthropologist can make [to the history of religions] is to illuminate by analogies drawn from the living present the obscurities of ancient texts." He might have gone further toward concluding that if that "living present" were to be perceived as the contemporary or most recent summation of all the past historical temporal phases, then the anthropologist's analyses of contemporary socio-cultural complexes would also have important historical implications.

It appears in these regards that Tambiah attempted the alternative theory which the critiques of Marriott failed to provide but in terms of a socio-historical hypothesis on Buddhism in the village-religion of contemporary Buddhist South Asia. Tambiah (1970:370) particularly had in mind the study of village-religion in contemporary Thailand through which he hoped to "advance further in some respects" than those "editors managed to do" by adopting a more dynamic and less static structuralism in regard to "the higher literary and the lower popular" levels of the religion, and a more historical and less ahistorical interpretation in view of the long time-periods governing their developmental "shifts in principles and ideas." He admitted that developmental considerations of this kind might be less interesting and relevant for the anthropologist than they are for the orientalist, the Indologist, and the historian of religions. But, they are relevant inasmuch as theys presuppose that there is no "single unbroken tradition" accessible to the anthropologist, no static "levels," no permanently "consistent" and "clear cut" principles, but instead "periods, eras, continuities, and changes" indicating a structural fluidity which the anthropologist must recognize and admit into interpretations and explanations of the data if these are not to be unhistorical and even "naive."[13]

C. Modernization and Traditionalization in Singer's Interpretation of Urban Hinduism

Marriott's dualistic characterization of village-Hinduism was richly complemented by Milton Singer's sociological interpretation of urban-Hinduism. During seventeen years of theoretical studies and field researches in the socio-anthropology and history of Indian civilization and culture, Singer utilized Robert Redfield's concepts of "Great Tradition" and "Little Tradition", and McKim Marriott's concepts of "sanskritization" and "parochialization", in a distinctive interpretation and explanation of "Sanskritic Hinduism" in the popular religion espoused by the population of metropolitan Madras and its environs. The importance of Singer's contribution to the scientific study of religions is amply indicated by the numerous references to and citations of his monumental compilation of those studies in When a Great Tradition Modernizes (1972). Moreover, given the depth and scope of his structuralist and historical study of urban Hinduism, it is not surprising that it provided also a rich frame of reference for comparable theoretical and historical studies on urban Buddhism in South and Southeast Asia.

When a Great Tradition Modernizes is a chronologically-arranged collection of published papers interspersing theoretical discussions with field-research reports. These collectively display his usage of the concepts of the "Sanskritic-Hindu Great Tradition" and of the "little tradition" of popular Hinduism in a structuralistic representation, functional analysis, and historical interpretation of the Great Tradition/Little Tradition duality of popular Hinduism in modern-day Madras. However, he also intended his structural-functionalist exploration to serve a historical purpose by indicating contributive factors and features of earlier times behind the complexity of the present-day traditional religion of Madras HIndus. He thought that these factors could be interpreted as indicators of the cultural "linear and cyclical processes" through which a heterogenetic culture such as modern Hinduism might historically have developed.

In this regard, Singer (1972:250-271) followed up on an argument by A.L. Kroeber (1963:40) that each human culture has a composite historical growth effected by the reworking and integrative organization of borrowed cultural elements into a "distinctive over-all pattern or style," that is, by gradual "shifts" toward consistent and coherent "sub-patterns and sub-styles" in its respective spheres of philosophy, religion, literature, sculpture, painting, architecture, social organization, etc. The "total pattern" or "style" of the culture is accordingly, a complex organization comprising diverse component "sub-styles." Moreover, while the general character of the culture is shaped by the holistic totality of these component "sub-styles," each sub-style has also contributed both unique features and a generative potentiality for further organic developments of the culture.[14]

Using the popular Hinduism espoused by the majority population of Madras as his model, Singer (1972:225-226) structurally represented the typical "compound and complex" socio-culture as a dualized whole which has a "high level" dimension or "great Tradition of the reflective few" and a "low level" or "little tradition" of "the unreflective many." These "levels" are communicationally interlinked with each other. Moreover, it is possible to identify the functional interrelations and the historical factors and conditions behind the two traditions.

Two principal historical and cultural factors are: (i) the social organizations which exist for the transmission of the "Great Tradition" which, in Hinduism, are the "literati" or "intellectual specialists," the "brahmanical schools," and the temples; and (ii) the predeterminants of the current phase of the civilization and socio-cultural development indicating whether or not it is in the "primary" or "orthogenetic" phase of its development - in which the indigenous "Great Tradition" is still "essentially homogenous with the Little Tradition" - or in "the secondary phase" where an alien or external "Great Tradition" has impinged upon or has become superimposed upon the primary tradition. In this regard, the primary tradition has undergone the "heterogenetic change" which alien civilizational contacts and infusions of foreign cultural elements effect in a culture.[15]

Singer developed these distinctions through a discussion with M.N. Śrinivas and McKim Marriott on whether or not any normative "Great Tradition" civilizational macrocosm can really exist by itself or is solely a conceptual system drawn by social scientists. Singer pointed out that a "primary" or singular "Great Tradition" civilization never really existed by itself in ancient India. Instead, the hypothetical "Great Tradition" of "Sanskritic-Hinduism" has coexisted with various "little tradition" subsystems within a stable complex of institutions, value-systems and other components of an heterogenetic civilization.

Singer's point, implies of course, the corresponding conditions for Buddhism in South Asia where no "Great Tradition" of Theravāda Buddhism can have existed independently of a contemporaneous "Little Tradition" civilizational system. Against the inclination in Obeyesekere and the majority of social scientists interested in Buddhist South Asian religions toward recognizing a distinct historic "Great Tradition" entity, Singer showed that Theravāda Buddhism can only be realistically perceived as one among several conceptually distinguishable components of a socio-cultural complex comprising also other Great Tradition subsystems as well as "Little Tradition" sub-systems. This "larger socio-culture complex" has also diverse local and regional variations in the respective "Theravāda Buddhist countries" of South and Southeast Asia.

But Singer did not follow through on his denial of the supposition that a conceptually adumbrated and hypothetically generalized "Great Tradition" of Sanskritic Hinduism might have had a distinct historic existence in the past. He nevertheless made the point that, throughout the entirety of India's civilizational history, there has been no single, uniform brahmanical tradition displaying a model "style of life" or pattern of values but instead, several contemporaneous brahmanical traditions reflecting diverse value-systems "whose precise content and . . . relative rank . . . [have varied] with time and [also with] locality." In this connection, Singer rejected the hypotheses presented by Staal (1963:261-275) and by V. Raghavan (1956) on the historical formation of a prototypical

Sanskritic-Hindu "Great Tradition" and its transformations "through contacts with regional and local socio-cultural [little] traditions." He also denied that they provided more plausible interpretations of the complex dual process of "Indianization" or "Sanskritization" and "modernization" or "westernization" than Srinivas had presented through his theory of "sanskritization" in the religion and socio-culture of the Coorgs of South India. Singer's sophisticated representation of the dynamics of continuity and change in the history of Hinduism shows his perceptive insight into the subtle "adaptational strategies" through which "continuity" and "transformation" intertwined in the historical development of Hinduism. His empirically sounder historical theory improved upon the current classical theory of static "traditional societies" becoming displaced by "dynamic" modern ones, and upon current historical theories of a linear evolution of monolithic "Great Traditions" unaffected by aboriginal and indigenous traditions encountered during their expansion beyond mainland India.

A crucial concern in When a Great Tradition Modernizes (1972) is the effects of modernity and modernization upon the interrelation of the "Great Tradition" and "Little Tradition" components of a socio-cultural system such as Hinduism. Singer's interest in modernization was sociological in regard to "whether continuing modernization would totally transform the structure and organization of Sanskritic Hinduism." But it also carried explicit historical overtones inasmuch as the question of modernistic cultural adaptation is also a question of the repeated contemporizing role of modernization behind the sequence of structural transformations which comprise the histories of "Great

Tradition" metasystems such as Sanskritic-Hinduism and Theravāda Buddhism.

On this matter, Singer rejected the opinions within his scientific community that "continuing modernization" eventually brings about the total transformation of a tradition, or cannot do so because there are traditional beliefs and institutions which are "incompatible with modernity," or that a total transformation comes about whenever the traditional features are fully eliminated by the traditional societies. He argued from "the continuing coexistence and mutual adaptations of India's cultural traditions - Great and Little - and modernity" that these do not indicate an "inevitable and linear transformation of a traditional society into a modern one," nor "the unchanging and obstructive persistence of a traditional society and culture." Their modernization does not come about through an abandoning of its traditionality. Instead, from "the long run telescopic perspective of culture history," the transformation appears as a combination of unity with continuity which is the pre-condition for adaptive change in any "historic" tradition. What we call "modernity", therefore, is another name for "contemporary forces"; and by "modernization" is meant the historic tradition's adaptations to conditions generating those "contemporary forces." In this light, modern Buddhism in contemporary South and Southeast Asia is the tradition's contemporizing adaptation to contemporary conditions and forces; it is the present historic phase culminating centuries of Buddhism's substantive growth and geographical expansion in South Asia.

Singer also explained that the word "modernization" is used by historians and sociologists in an indicative and not in a definitional sense. The word is intended to mean "contemporization" or "adjustment to contemporary forces," particularly in the context of the recent impact upon Third World countries of urbanization, politicization, industrialization, western science, and western education. Singer (1972:282f.) specifically considered the manner in which individuals and groups in contemporary South Asia have adapted their traditional ecclesiastical institutions, ritual structures, and belief-systems to recently impacting Western socio-cultural systems. Nevertheless, he concluded that, when all of the adaptations are set within a chronological sequence, they illustrate principles for an historical theory of modernizing socio-cultural change, and for a general theory of religious historical development combining both socio-anthropological and academic-historical perspectives. This socio-historical perspective presupposes that the structures of a religion are never static nor final at any stage of a religion's history. Even the most "traditional" of the great religions have been centuries in the making and continue to unfold beyond their primal and later canonical, commentarial and hermeneutical literary traditions. Any canonical tradition, accordingly, presents seemingly "modernistic" ideas and teachings through developing ideological linkages with impinging alien traditions which leave untouched the core elements of its normative character and canonicity.

Singer (1972:235) also explained this adaptational modernization in terms of the "inner or essential core" by which the intrinsic identity and authenticity of the tradition are protected and sustained despite the tradition's subjection to the powerful external influences. Yet, this central "core" has an organic pliancy enabling it to absorb innovations from its cultural environment through reconstructional and adaptational mechanisms which accommodate alien elements

and make obsolescent any traditional elements which
cannot be "technically modernized" nor functionally
updated.

Applied to the history of Buddhism in South Asia,
Singer's summary (1972: 259, 366) on the impact of
modernization on "traditional religions" indicates the
following generalizations about the history of Buddhist
development in South and Southeast Asia.

1. Buddhism in South and Southeast Asia has always
been a self-modernizing tradition through
adaptational responsiveness to changes in its
socio-cultural environment especially to the more
recent innovations of urbanization, politicization,
etc.

2. This adaptational capacity, however, has never
damaged the canonical "core" of Buddhist
traditional institutions, values, and beliefs even
though these have been continuously restructured
under the influence of impacting alien socio-
cultural innovations.

3. The historical "restructuring" of this "core"
has appeared most extensively in the Buddhist
ritual system, and least extensively within the
domestic systems of the Buddhist tradition.

4. The historic outcome of this restructuring of
Buddhism has been a "linear" historical
transformation through "experimentation with . . .
and gradual incorporation of innovative changes . .
of foreign and indigenous origin into an indigenous
culture" which, in consequence, is both
"traditional" and "modern".

5. This receptivity for innovations has determined
the fact and the pace of Buddhist historical
development due to the nature of the innovations-
in regard to their amenability or non-acceptability

to the tradition, the <u>forcefulness</u> of the innovations, the <u>syncretistic adaptability</u> of the tradition, its <u>absorbability</u> of new and borrowed elements, and the <u>strength</u> of the "adaptive strategies" or "modes of adaptation" forced into operation by the innovations themselves yet within the constraints imposed by the tradition.

6. The syncretistic adaptivity of Buddhism in South and Southeast Asia has shaped its history through "a highly selective process of borrowing and innovation" reflecting a self-perpetuating momentum in the Buddhist tradition.

7. Since, in South and Southeast Asia, the principal mainstream traditional religion has been Theravāda Buddhism, its history can be interpreted in terms of the restructurings of its "core" through the adaptive mechanisms and strategies which have effected its gradual incorporation of religious innovations introduced from: (i) the aboriginal, "pre-Buddhist" environment of South and Southeast Asia; (ii) the impact of recent alien forces and traditions; and (iii) the diversificational innovations of the "elitist", "popular", rural, urban, monastic, lay, regional, national, and "political" forms of the religion which have unfolded throughout the period of its expansion and establishment as the mainline religion of Buddhist South Asia.

In these conclusions are the principles, which have emerged in Redfield's, Marriott's, and Singer's theoretical presentations in the sociology of religions, and by which the socio-scientific studies of Buddhism in Srī Laṅka, Burma, and Thailand can be compared and evaluated specifically in regard to the character and

historic development of the Theravāda Buddhist religion
in South and Southeast Asia.

Chapter Two. Great Tradition and Little Tradition
Theravāda Buddhism in Śrī Laṅkā

The history of Theravāda Buddhism in South and Southeast Asia comprises the collective influences of "Sanskritic-Hindu" or "Brahmanical" civilization and socio-culture in mainland and further India, of Mahāyāna Buddhism, and of the aboriginal "pre-Buddhist" socio-cultural traditions of South and Southeast Asia. In Ceylon, the history of Theravāda Buddhism is the process of adaptational transformations which has occurred through the acculturational dialectic described by Marriott as the "parochialization" or indigenization of India's exported Buddhism and the "buddhaization" of the indigenous, pre-Buddhist, aboriginal religions. This process indicates that the history of Buddhism in South and Southeast Asia, including the fortunes of Theravāda Buddhism in particular, are more complex than current "histories" of Theravāda Buddhism might lead one to expect.

A. Buddhist Cultural Diffusion from Mainland India into Southeast Asia

Sociologists interested in Theravāda Buddhism in South and Southeast Asia drew their socio-historical interpretations from the extant traditional historiographies, chronicles, annals, inscriptions, monuments, and artistic representations of Buddhist beliefs, doctrines, and institutions commissioned by early and later Buddhist kings, merchants, and other wealthy patrons of Buddhism as well as upon contemporary socio-anthropological data, and also from an abundance of secondary-source historical materials and archeological descriptions of the religions or pre-historic, pre-Buddhist, and Buddhist South and Southeast Asia. Both the primary and the secondary sources indicate that the history of Buddhism in Southeast Asia

began as a diffusional extension of the socio-cultural
history of India. This comprises, as Mortimer Wheeler
(1968:137) indicated, the diffusion of an Indus-valley
urban culture throughout India around 1500 B.C., the
spread of the Gangetic civilization after 500 B.C., and
the movement of the Indian Buddhist civilization along
the Gangetic and the Deccan "corridors" linking India
with South and Southeast Asia from the third century
B.C. where, as William Kirk (1975) put it, the interplay
of natural and cultural environments effected the
general "transformation of cultural complexes by trans-
regional adaptations." These adaptations, however,
comprised more than the ideological reinterpretations of
the Sanskritic-Hindu and Indian Buddhist metaphysics,
cosmology, and theistic supernaturalism enshrined in the
sacred texts preserved by their professional classes of
priestly and monastic communicators. They included
socio-cultural adaptations also at the popular and folk
levels of the regions and communities into which those
Indian Hindu and Buddhist systems were transmitted.

Nevertheless, contrary to William Kirk's
indications on "The Role of India in the Diffusion of
Cultures (1975), those acculturative transformations of
the Indian ideological and social systems, due to the
interplay of changing natural and cultural environments
along the path of their spatial diffusion, were not
passive "happenings". Adherents and communicators
within the successive geographical areas of their
spatial expansion "indigenized" or "parochialized" the
imported systems and thereby made them integral features
of their syncretic cultures and civilization.[1]

The mechanisms and stages of this syncretistic
acculturational process are indicated by Kirk (1975:20).
He explained that, in regard to "long term diffusion

processes," one should specially note: (i) certain characteristics of those processes, such as the various obstacles and facilitators of the diffusion; (ii) "the phenomenon of cultural transformation whereby elements are transformed in the course of diffusion by adaptation to local physical and cultural environments through which they are passing"; (iii) the spatial and temporal "limits of diffusion" inasmuch as "innovation waves" occur in "irregular, jerky, forward movements," they appear sometimes "static" as though "lacking the power of further penetration," but then, "as though the system had been re-energized, there occurs a sudden leap forward to new frontiers"; (iv) "the influence of contrasting environments on the diffusion of cultures and the spatial behaviour of various communities as culture bearers"; and (v) the "end-product" since this "may appear to be very different from the element at the outset of its journey."

These general features of cultural diffusion in Kirk's exposition are applicable to the spacial expansion and temporal growth of Buddhism beyond mainland India. It indicates the kinds and ranges of the transformations which Buddhism must have undergone along the corridors of its spacial expansion within and beyond India during the centuries prior to the composition of the Buddhist chronicles and the historiographical legends concerning the introducion of Buddhism into Ceylon from the second century B.C. Furthermore, Kirk's intimation of the difference between the "end-product" and the primary forms of the expanding tradition suggests a different form of Theravāda Buddhism espoused by the Sinhalese contrasting with the Indian form of Theravāda Buddhism which the emperor Aśoka had formally introduced into Śrī Laṅkā according

to the Sinhalese Buddhist chronicles. Nevertheless, it
can be assumed that the Theravāda Buddhism of India had
already acquired folk dimensions and features of Indian
supernaturalistic and animistic religion centuries prior
to its outward migration from India, and that these
features must have provided the links and
identifications connecting the folk-Buddhism of India
with the pre-Buddhist Sinhalese aboriginal folk-
religion. Moreoever, the concept of "cultural layers"
indicates the possibility of "peeling back" accretional
layers from centuries of popular Buddhist growth in
mainland and further India for the purpose of
recapitulating the history of Buddhist transformations
in South Asia.

However, before this retrospective historical
reconstruction is made to qualify the older projective
academic historicism on Buddhism, two observations on
"cultural diffusion" made by Kirk (1976:33) warrant
prior attention. The first is the syncretic
responsivity of aboriginal peoples to alien imported
socio-cultural systems. In Buddhist South Asia, none of
India's expanding socio-cultural systems - including
their ideologies, ritual systems, and institutions-
could have taken root and flourished in the new socio-
cultural environments unless they were popularly
"absorbed, reorganized and transformed . . . to meet the
needs" of local peoples. But the resultant "cultural
package" of the host peoples is expectedly different
from, and could even be barely recognizable from, the
tradition originally introduced from outside.

The second observation is the inherent
"conservatism" of "traditional cultures" manifested by
their "ability . . . to preserve a cultural element,
virtually in a state of suspended animation, for long

periods of time until conditions are ripe for its rejuvenation" in later urbanized, politicized, and other ideological, institutional, etc. socio-cultural forms.

In both of these observations the history of Theravāda Buddhism in mainland India and further South and Southeast Asia is interpretable in terms of the first process of syncretic adoption of its supernaturalistic and animistic components into the "popular religion" of South Asia's majority of peasant-folk, and in terms of the second process of its urbanized rejuvenation and eventual re-exportation back along the corridors of its cultural diffusion into modern India and beyond into Europe and illustrated by the recent history of the "neo-Buddhism" of the Sinhalese Mahābodhi Society.

B. Redfieldian Concepts in the Socio-History of Sinhalese Buddhism

Although Redfield's associates in the Chicago School largely focussed their sociological disquisitions upon the spacial interrelations of the "Great Tradition" and "little tradition" components of the "Sanskritic-Hindu civilization" of mainland India, social scientists later applied their scientific insights to the Buddhist great tradition civilization and socio-culture of South Asia. There, McKim Marriott's concepts of "universalization" and "parochialization" explained the complexity of contemporary Buddhist South Asian religions in socio-historical terms of the integration of the imported Theravāda Buddhist "Great Tradition" with the indigenous, aboriginal, pre-Buddhist religions of South and Southeast Asia's peasant-folk. Yet they did not follow up on Singer's leads for drawing out the historical implications of this acculturative absorption of an imported alien tradition into a local and older, aboriginal one, particularly in regard to Theravāda Buddhism. This was even prevented by their interpretational acquiescences to the prestigious current historical view of the Theravāda Buddhism of Buddhist South Asia's elites of scholars and intellectuals which led them, in turn, to attribute the "Theravāda" designation only to those parts of the regional Buddhisms which could be obviously identified with the ancient canonical and historiographical traditions of Buddhism.[2] This criterion inevitably led to a contrasting of "non-Theravāda" and "non-Buddhist" religion categories with "Theravāda Buddhism". "Popular Buddhism", "Mahāyāna Buddhism", "Brāhmanism", "Supernaturalism", and "Animism" were distinguished as competing contemporaneous traditions which never converged into a Buddhist hybrid religious complexity in the "Theravāda Buddhist countries" of South and Southeast Asia.

The preclusion of non-Theravāda religions from Theravāda Buddhism was not implied by the Redfieldian concepts and theory of peasant socio-cultures which represented the integrational development of rural and urban cultures and societies. On the other hand, the peasant socio-cultural paradigm positively advanced the sociological researches on Buddhism in South Asia during the nineteen-sixties and seventies. The published researches indicate the revolutionizing impact of the Redfieldian concepts and theory on the scientific interpretation of the Buddhist socio-historic reality in Ceylon and the rest of Buddhist South Asia. They show the sociological confrontations with the current textual-historical scholarship on Theravāda Buddhism during the two-decade period unfolding new insights into the complexity of its popular as well as its elite or normative forms and manifestations specifically on account of an understanding of the acculturational mechanisms behind the conjoining of South and Southeast Asia's ancient animistic and supernaturalistic religions with imported varieties of Buddhism. The syncretical and acculturational processes of "parochialization" and "buddhaization" which Marriott described were made to explain the integration of an imported Theravāda Buddhism and the pre-Buddhist aboriginal religions of South and Southeast Asia, including the mechanisms and processes by which those ancient, aboriginal religions became buddhistically-authorized during the earlier stages of Theravāda Buddhism's acculturation in South and Southeast Asia.

The illustrations of these buddhaizing processes in the "Sinhalese religion" area appeared in a succession of socio-anthropological studies during the nineteen-sixties and seventies. These ranged from the sophisticated expositions of the normative character and role of Theravāda Buddhism in the Sinhalese religion by Ganganath Obeyesekere (1963) to the highly dichotomized representations of the Sinhalese religion by Ames (1964) and the distinctive analytical interpretations of the urban and politicized forms of Theravāda Buddhism by Hans-Deiter Evers (1973) and Heinz Bechert (1978). They also reflect the interpretational liability of the Redfield-Marriott dichotomy applied to the religions of Buddhist South Asia both for a scientific interpretation of Theravāda Buddhism's character and historical development in South and Southeast Asia.

C. Normative and Historic Buddhism in the Religion of Ceylon

In "The Great Tradition and the Little Tradition in the Perspective of Sinhalese Buddhism" (1963),

Obeyesekere declared his intention as being "to examine
critically the utility, from a methodological point of
view, of the approach to peasant culture outlined by the
late Robert Redfield in . . . Peasant Society and
Culture" [1956] and to inquire "how useful" Redfield's
concepts and socio-cultural theory might be "for
understanding the nature of peasant culture" such as is
found in the rural "little community" of Ceylon. He
indicated a procedure along the lines of investigation
applied by McKim Marriott to a named "little community"
of north India. He presupposed that the "typical
Sinhalese little community" has a socio-culture which is
a microcosm of the macrocosmic Buddhist "Great
Tradition" civilization of South and Southeast Asia. He
perceived the Sinhalese "little community" accordingly
as a laboratory whose various componential and systemic
relationships - indicated and described by Redfield and
Marriott - could be investigated and examined, and the
interpretational applications of the "Redfield-Marriott
dichotomy" of "Great Tradition" and "Little Tradition"
tested against the complexity of contemporary Sinhalese
rural and pesant-folk religion.

Yet Obeyesekere's approach to the Sinhalese
religious totality began as a critique of the Redfield-
Marriott dichotomy itself particularly in regard to
recent misuses of its concepts for the hypothetical
relationship of "Great Tradition" religious systems and
its "Little Traditon" religious elements and features.[3]
He nevertheless assumed that "the Redfield-Marriott
dichotomy" is applicable both to the Sinhalese religious
system and to other religious complexes which
historically developed in other regions of Theravada
Buddhist South Asia provided that it was subjected to
several necessary modifications. He even acknowledged

the applicability of Redfield's concepts of "Great Tradition" and "Little Tradition" to the religious complexity in Buddhist South Asia but thought that Marriott's general sociological theory of "secondary civilizational development," and his explanation of its acculturative "parochializational" and "sanskritizational" mechanisms, needed to be re-interpreted to fit the particular socio-cultural context of Buddhist South Asia where they could correctly explain Theravāda Buddhism's relationships with the "popular religion" of South Asia's majority of Theravāda Buddhists.[4]

On the other hand, Obeyesekere's critique of the Redfield-Marriott dichotomy indicates an unclear comprehension of the complexity which the mechanisms of acculturative interaction and other integrative "civilizational processes" generated in the peasant socio-cultures. Obeyesekere mistakenly thought that Redfield and Marriott had perceived the "little community" and its socio-culture as "a composite structure consisting of a [distinguishable] great and little tradition" as though "the great tradition is, in fact, institutionalized . . in the little community." He argued against them by contending that it is not the whole of the "Buddhist Great Tradition" that is institutionalized in the peasant socio-culture of contemporary rural Ceylon, but only part of it. But Redfield and Marriott had only envisaged the "Great Tradition" and the "Little Tradition" as useful concepts for interpretively representing the complexity of "little community" socio-cultures, not as distinct empirical entities which could be historically explained as being entirely or partially appropriated by a real socio-culture.

Nevertheless, in Obeyesekere's representation of the religion of the Sinhalese Buddhist "little community" the concepts served Obeyesekere's recognition of it as being an eclectic compound of "Great Tradition" and "Little Tradition" religious elements and features producing the hybrid "popular Buddhism" traditionally followed by Ceylon's Theravāda Buddhist peasant-majority. He perceived this hybridization of the religion moreover as a factor of its historic unity. The Sinhalese do not simultaneously espouse a duality or plurality of religions. The Sinhalese Buddhist population has one religion. But this comprises a functionally-integrated complex of religions which were once historically distinct but became only partially integrated. This composite "Sinhalese religion", accordingly, is properly perceived neither as Theravāda Buddhism nor as "the folk-animism". The hybrid religion is "Buddhist" by adoption and authorization but has many significant "non-Buddhist" features. He concluded from these observations that it is inappropriate for socio-anthropologists to adopt the recommendation of Dumont and Pocock (1958:39-40) that the socio-culture of the "little community" should be perceived as a unified "little tradition" which is historically distinct from a contemporaneous Theravāda Buddhist "Great Tradition".

On the other hand, he arbitrarily deleted the appellation of "Theravāda Buddhism" from this hybrid religion of the Sinhalese "little community". This in turn denied the possible recognition of the religion of Ceylon's peasant Theravāda Buddhists as a local or regional mode of Theravāda Buddhism. Instead, he represented the religion of Ceylon's Buddhists in terms of three traditions comprising Theravāda Buddhism, Sinhalese Religion, and pre-Buddhist Folk Religion.

This represented the "Sinhalese religion" not as a syncretic amalgam of Theravāda Buddhism and the pre-Buddhist folk-religion but as an unintegrated temporal conjunction of religious pieces, thereby leaving intact two distinctive historical religions of Theravada Buddhism - the imported "Great Tradition" - and the aboriginal "Little Tradition". Moreover, the idea of a distinct and intact Theravāda Buddhist "Great Tradition" was important for Obeyesekere who became more concerned with explaining the normative role of Theravāda Buddhism in relation to the popular Sinhalese religion than with the popular adoption of Theravāda Buddhism in rural Buddhist South Asia in Marriott's terms of its parochialization and acculturation with the folk-religion stream of Ceylon's peasant population.

In the end, Obeyesekere's representation of the scenario of Ceylon's Buddhist religion was strongly dualistic. He presented Theravāda Buddhism as an abstraction from the mainstream of popular religious belief and practice and imputed to it a prestigious, specialized, yet limited functional role as the normative religion serving as the source of ideal values and ideas for the whole of Buddhist South Asia. He set it above the diverse regional and local Buddhisms of Ceylon, Burma, Thailand, and other "Theravāda Buddhist countries" of South and Southeast Asia as being the authenticating source of their "Buddhist" identity and ideal values and doctrines, yet never as an integral part of their "traditional" religion.

Yet the purpose behind Obeyesekere's representation of this dualistic scenario was to correct "several pitfalls and misconceptions" which had appeared in writings of contemporary scholars on the patterns of religious development within the "little communities" of

Buddhist South Asia. He thought that Ryan (1958) and
Kaufman (1960) had erroneously assumed that "peasant
beliefs derived from the great tradition" can be
"equated with the great tradition itself" rather than
being only selected elements of the great tradition.[5]
Ryan appears to have perceived the religion of a named
village as a dual system forged by infusions of "the
wonderful world" of Buddhism with the aboriginal
supernaturalistic world of local gods and demons.
Kaufman had presented a more complex view of the
religion of a Thai village "little community" which he
supposed is a triple system comprising the imported
brahmanical "Great Tradition", the regionally developed
Hīnayāna "Great Tradition", and the animistic "little
tradition" of spirit-worship. Obeyesekere objected that
Ryan had mistaken a behavioural distinction for an
historical one. He had supposed that functionally
distinguishable features and components of the village
religious-ritual could be historically arranged in a
sequence of ritual-changes which could be historically
interpreted as the outworkings of syncretistic and
functionalist processes which produced the hybrid
complex of "Sinhalese religion". Obeyesekere rejected
both Kaufman's and Ryan's conclusions as being contrary
to historical and empirical fact. They had been misled
by the Redfield-Marriott dichotomy into empirically and
historically ungrounded stratifications of the Sinhalese
religious complex. Obeyesekere (1963:141) also judged
J.E. de Young's work (1955) to be another
missapplication of Redfield's and Marriott's
externalistic concepts of socio-cultural "levels",
"layers", or "strata" to the internal organization of
the religion and socio-cultures of the "little
communities" of Buddhist South Asia. Against de Young,

he insisted that animism, Brāhmanism, and Buddhism do not occur respectively as the lower, middle, and upper "layers" or "strata" of the religion because there are no real strata in the religion practiced by the peasant-folk.[6]

Obeyesekere particularly objected to peasant-folk religion being "Animism", and to the notion that an "animistic layer" became superimposed upon a Buddhist "higher culture" in the belief-system of the peasant-folk. He particularly criticized de Young's perpetuation of this earlier anthropological viewpoint which labelled the Buddhist South Asian folk-religion as "Animism" on account of the prominence in it of beliefs, practices, and myths about spirits having magical powers and capable of being manipulated through "magical rituals." Obeyesekere rejected the notion of "Animistic religion" as a "label" invented by anthropologists yet "rarely . . . clearly defined," and serving as a convenient term for the collectivity of folk beliefs and customs which the anthropologist "did not fully comprehend or was impatient with."[7] The "animist label" concealed rather than displayed the real unity of the religion of the peasant-folk as a local type of folk-Buddhism.

Obeyesekere's criticisms of contemporary socio-anthropological "misrepresentations" of the religion of Ceylon's peasant-folk prefaced his own conception of that religion and his own perception of the social scientist's task in regard to it. He perceived "the little community" in Buddhist South Asia as "the Buddhist little community" and as having a "Buddhist little tradition." He perceived the anthropologist's task as explaining this "Buddhist little tradition" sociologically in structural and systemic terms of the

integral "levels" of belief-patterns, and in functional
terms of their interconnections with the historic "Great
Tradition" of "Theravāda Buddhism".

Obeyesekere also thought that a systemic-analysis
"approach" to the religious complexity of the Buddhist
"little community" would present a scientifically
sounder exposition of "the existent reality" of the
"little religious tradition" than was currently found in
anthropological writings.   It would display the
character of the religion as a distinctive unity in
which "the speculations of orthodoxy" have neither an
equivalence, nor a part. He also supposed that an
empirical and conceptual differentiation of this "little
tradition" Buddhism from the concurrent Theravāda
Buddhist "Great Tradition" would facilitate an
anthropological explanation of the "little tradition" of
the "little community" in Buddhist South Asia by
bringing to light its structural and functional
"linkages" with the "vastly different" Great Tradition
of Buddhism with which it is historically connected.
Although he recognized that the Sinhalese Buddhist
"little tradition" was beyond complete verbal definition
and explanation, he assumed that its anthropological
representation and explanation through systematic
characterizations and analyses of its component
structural systems such as its theistic pantheon, its
mythic ideology, its world view, its ritual framework,
etc., and their arrangement into "serried levels" would
scientifically display its real proximity with the
Theravāda Buddhist "Great Tradition" in Ceylon.

Obeyesekere's resultant characterization of the
traditional religion in contemporary Buddhist Ceylon
amply demonstrates his methodological and
interpretational sophistication in the socio-

anthropology of religion. Moreover, the arguments by which he defended his interpretational positions make it difficult to find fault with his conclusions. Nevertheless, his interpretation can be challenged on several empirical grounds. Primarily, his dualistic distinction between "Theravāda Buddhism" and "Sinhalese religion" presupposes that there are features of the one which do not belong to the other. For example, the doctrinal and philosophical features belong to Theravāda Buddhism and the theistic and supernaturalistic features ·belong to Sinhalese religion. Obeyesekere (1963:145) failed to provide sufficient empirical evidence supporting his observation that Sinhalese religion is a theistic system while Theravāda Buddhism is "a philosophical and doctrinal system" which lacks any "theistic component" and "hierarchy of supernaturals."[8] The supposition is indicated for the scholastic Theravāda Buddhism by the Abhidhamma-sūtra literature; but it is not supported by the Nikayas whose diverse perspectives on the Buddha, his works, and his teaching display both philosophical, supernaturalistic, animistic, and theistic features in canonical Buddhism.[9]

Obeyesekere's distinction between Sinhalese religion and Theravāda Buddhism denies the real unity of the religion of Ceylon's Theravāda Buddhist population. In their religious understanding there is no concrete or substantive distinction between the two. Their "Sinhalese religion" is Theravāda Buddhism. In the same manner the popular Burmese and the Thai versions of Theravāda Buddhism comprise respectively their "Burmese religion" and "Thai religion", and so on throughout Theravāda Buddhist South Asia. Accordingly, the unity of the Theravāda Buddhist religion of the Sinhalese overrules Obeyesekere's assumption that the Sinhalese espouse two religions or even two Buddhisms. It also discredits his suppposition that Theravāda Buddhism is a philosophical and doctrinal system which lacks theistic and supernaturalistic components, and also his conclusion that Sinhalese religion is a supernaturalistic system which needed Theravāda Buddhism for its philosophical and doctrinal superstructure. The empirical evidence on contemporary Sinhalese Buddhism does not justify Obeyesekere's historical conclusion in regard to the contemporary end-result of Theravāda Buddhist development in Ceylon and the rest of Buddhist South Asia. It is not evident that Theravāda Buddhism survived outside of its syncretical adoption and popularization in Buddhist South Asia. It could not have survived for centuries solely in a transcendental relation to the "popular Buddhist" and aboriginal "non-Buddhist" religions of the peasant population, but only as an integral part of the folk-religion.[10]

On the other hand, the high point of Obeyesekere's interpretive exposition of the duality of Ceylon's traditional religion was his working out of the functionalistic interconnections of the conceptually-distinguished systems. In this regard, Obeyesekere (1963:147ff.) employed the Redfieldian concept and theory of "communicational interlinkages" to explain how certain common ideas, themes, motifs, and doctrines-such as Karma - are functionalistically complementive for both systems. Through the shared concept of Karma, for example, "the Sinhalese theory of causation" provides theoretical and practical explanations for the "events or human fortunes" which the Sinhalese Buddhist laity experience. The Theravāda Buddhist philosophy of Karma rationalizes the popular religion based on notions of "merit" and "demerit", the popular doctrines and ideas of divine benevolent or punitive intervention, the action of malevolent and beneficent planetary influences, the afflictions of demons, and other "contradictory frames of reference" utilized for interpreting and explaining natural predicaments.[11]

Obeyesekere also noticed that aspects of Sinhalese Buddhist ideology and behaviour which seem to outside "observers" as being "logically contradictory" are nevertheless practically reconciled by "insiders." The seemingly contradictory interpretations through which they understand adverse circumstances and untoward events and experiences are not "contradictory" from their viewpoint. For although "Western observers and Buddhist intellectuals are often puzzled by the addiction to magic and a polytheistic pantheon in societies with a great tradition of Theravāda Buddhism, with its devaluation of magic and supernatural beings," their bewilderment disappears when the "addiction" is viewed as an expression of complementary modes of dealing with adverse conditions and forces unpredictably influencing human life, and NOT as the contradictory approaches of Sinhalese Buddhism and "Theravāda Buddhism."

But a higher intellectual resolution of the "contradictions" lies in the recognition of "Sinhalese Buddhism" and "Theravāda Buddhism" as lesser and larger versions of the same thing, that is, not as TWO religions but as the one religion of Theravāda Buddhism having its higher or ideological "level" of expression and its lower or pragmatical "level" of meaning and expression. From this perspective, the contradictory modes of handling adverse conditions are reflections of the diverse expressions of the complex, polylithic, or pluriform Theravāda Buddhist religion traditionally

espoused by the larger majority of Ceylon's Theravāda
Buddhists. In this light, Obeyesekere's insistence that
"Sinhalese Buddhism cannot be equated with Theravāda" is
defensible only if Theravāda Buddhism is <u>abstractly</u>
perceived as an ideology or a doctrinal system
communicated by a professional Theravāda Buddhist elite.
It is not tenable if Sinhalese Theravāda Buddhism is
recognized as an historic complex which has arisen
through syncretistic processes which have fused the
Theravāda Buddhist religion of ancient India with the
pre-Buddhist and non-Buddhist aboriginal religions of
Ceylon.

In this light, Obeyesekere's distinctions between
"Sinhalese religion" and "Theravāda Buddhism" lack the
empirical underpinnings of an historically valid
interpretation of the character and development of
Buddhism in śrī Laṅkā. His interpretation is also
complicated by his recognition in "Sinhalese religion"
of a substantial "Theravāda Buddhist" component, or a
complex of Theravāda features and elements, yet not
substantive enough to have 'theravāda-ized' the total
religious metasystem of the Sinhalese. Despite his
contention that the unified tradition of Ceylon's
majority-population of Theravāda Buddhists comprises
stratificatory "levels" of normative and non-normative
religion interconnected with Theravāda Buddhism through
"shared concepts" and "ritual exchanges," he
nevertheless denied recognition of this composite
totality as "Sinhalese Theravāda Buddhism" or the form
which Theravāda Buddhism had historically assumed in
Ceylon. In effect, he denied that Theravāda Buddhism is
"the religion" of the Sinhalese people even though these
have traditionally regarded themselves as "Theravāda
Buddhists". He conceded that they "subscribe to it

ideally" to the extent that they "pay lip service to the great tradition in its entirety," that they draw from it concepts and meanings indicating that Theravāda Buddhism constitutes its normative "frame of reference," and that these inform their values and make sense of the fortunes and misfortunes of their daily life. But he did not concede that these collectively add up to their espousal of Theravāda Buddhism.

All this is because Obeyesekere had adopted the precedent set by the academic historians that the real ·Theravāda Buddhism of Ceylon is the ideal Buddhism which is shared by all the Theravāda Buddhist countries of South Asia. This is "the Buddhism of the monastery" administered by the Buddhist monks. Beside it, "the Buddhism of the village" served by "the priests of the lower cults" is not the Buddhist tradition couched in scriptures and commentaries "written in Pali" but is an ancient oral tradition expressed in myth, legend, and dramatic performances during popular festivals. He also contrasted their respective ancient institutions, that is, the monasteries of the "Sanghika Theravāda Buddhist sects" and their regional chapters, and the temples with their shrines in which the priestly cults are practiced.[12]

But Obeyesekere appears to have confused conceptual distinctions with historical differentiations. The contrastive ministries and concepts of the monastic and the priestly systems reflect the symbolic and the pragmatical integrations of the religion of the monks and the religion of the laity. Elements which appear to be intrinsic to the canonical Theravāda Buddhism espoused by the Buddhist elites appear as functionalistically extrinsic popular expressions among the laity. In this regard, the relation of the

Theravāda Buddhist philosophical concept of Karma and the popular Buddhist theory of merit and demerit appear, in the light of McKim Marriott's theory of the "cyclical development of concepts" in socio-cultures, as the complementary levels of intellectual and popular appropriation and expression of a shared concept. This bi-level sharing occurs over the totality of shared ideas, beliefs, practices, and institutions connecting the religion of the monks with the religion of the laity:[13] The complementarity of the two "levels" over-rules the empiralization of "contradictions" between the monastic and lay appropriations of the Buddhist tradition drawn by social scientists.[14] Obeyesekere's representation of the contrastive forms of shared concepts as "paradoxes" stemming from the unequal yoking of similar Theravāda Buddhist and folk-religious beliefs and practices softened his view of the contradictoriness of the systems. His idea of complementary "levels" of functional appropriation also harmonized the "other-worldly" religion of Theravāda Buddhism's professional elites with the "this-worldly" religion of Theravāda Buddhism's laity, but unfortunately without recognizing the shared "Theravāda" identity of both religions.[15]

Even Obeyesekere's subtle and sophisticated exposition of the network of communicational and pragmatical linkages connecting the Theravāda Buddhist "Great Tradition" with the Sinhalese religious "Little Tradition" of the peasant population in the terminology of the Redfield-Marriott dichotomy accentuated the duality despite his admissions about the unity of the religion of Ceylon's Theravāda Buddhist peasant-majority. His conceptual distinctions between "Theravāda Buddhism" and "Sinhalese religion" presented a truncated version of the religion of Ceylon's Buddhist laity and a cerebral version of the religion of the Buddhist elites. This, in turn, paved the way for a sociological view of Theravāda Buddhism as "an incomplete religion" needing pragmatical supplementations from the non-Buddhist religion or from the "pre-Buddhist" religion of the masses. However, this deficiency in an otherwise empirically sound and historically valid account of the religion of Ceylon's Buddhists presented an occasion, and its agenda, for an wholistic scientific representation merging both "levels" of the Theravāda Buddhist religious system which his contemporaries - principally Michael Ames- and his immediate successors took up and followed through during the later nineteen-sixties and throughout the nineteen-seventies in their sociological studies of religion in Ceylon, Burma, and Thailand.

D. Supernaturalized Animism in Sinhalese Theravāda Buddhism

Michael Ames' representation of the Sinhalese religion set a standard for sociological research on religions during the nineteen-sixties and seventies. His work shaped comparable studies of urban Sinhalese Buddhism principally by Hans-Dieter Evers and Heinz Bechert, directly influenced systematic psychological representations and interpretations of the Burmese religion by Melford E. Spiro and the microscopic analyses of Thai rural-village supernaturalism and macroscopic surveys of Thai urban Buddhism by S.J. Tambiah.

Ames introduced his methodology for a systematic survey of the total Sinhalese religious system in an essay titled: "Magical Animism and Buddhism. A Structural Analysis of the Sinhalese Religious System" (1964). In it, Ames (1964:21) explained his approach as "the first attempt since Weber to subject a total religious system of Greater India to a systematic sociological analysis." The starting-point of this grandiose scheme was his observation that "the vast majority" of the Sinhalese are "Theravāda Buddhists" who also happen to "indulge in a rich array of magical-animist and other non-Buddhist practices." His opening statement accordingly presupposed the distinctions between "Buddhist" and "non-Buddhist" religious beliefs and practices simultaneously held and practiced by Sinhalese Buddhists. This distinction determined the dualistic shape of his systematic representation of the Sinhalese Religious totality according to the principal patterns of its component subsystems of religious belief and practice and of their functional interrelations.

Although Ames was a contemporary of Obeyesekere in Sinhalese-religion studies, they worked independently and produced strikingly different interpretations.[16] Although Ames' work was a singular application of the Redfield-Marriott dichotomy to a religion of Buddhist South Asia he drew substantially different conclusions about the relations in Sinhalese religion of "Buddhism" and "non-Buddhism". While he significantly advanced Obeyesekere's perceptions of the interrelation of the Theravāda Buddhist "Great Tradition" and the "Little Tradition" religion in the "little communities" of Ceylon, his work can also be read as a repudiation of the overly emphasized dichotomies in Obeyesekere's interpretation of the relation of canonical Theravāda Buddhism to the Sinhalese religion.

In "Magical Animism and Buddhism" (1964b:40), Ames emphasized that "there is no simple dichotomy between Great and Little Traditions, sophisticate and folk religions, urbanite and villager." He agreed that "dichotomy" does exist, but that this is between "Buddhism" and "non-Buddhism", and between "religion" and "non-religion", but not within the "religion" itself. The dichotomy is between "the sacred" and its soteriological utilizations and "the profane" or the non-religious magical rites and their pragmatical utilizations. In the religion, accordingly there is a functional dichotomy, not a substantive duality. Some of the religion's subsystemic components are directed toward soteriological goals; others pragmatically serve human needs.

But Ames also observed that the Sinhalese religious system on the whole is a "village-centered religious system." It is not "Buddhist" or a form of Buddhism, but has "a bias toward Buddhism" and is "Buddhist dominated." That village-system bows to "the religion of a Buddhist monkhood" which is "nation-wide rather than village-centered" and is the religion of "the dominant status group" in the Sinhalese religious system. Buddhism, accordingly, is not intrinsic to Sinhalese religion but is its principal religious adjunct. And, since it is exterior to the "Sinhalese religion," it cannot be recognized as part of the latter's definition. Moreover, like any other distinctive religion, Sinhalese Buddhism has an integrity, vitality, and historic life of its own. It is also both a soteriology and a social institution. As a soteriology, it is "other-worldly" or "sacred"; but as a social institution, it is "secular", that is, an expression of the contemporary Sinhalese socio-cultural world.

A crucial distinction in Ames' interpretation is his contrasts between the essential sacrality of Sinhalese Buddhism and the utilitarian secularity of the

Sinhalese religion. On the other hand, he sometimes also blurred his distinctions between the "sacred" and the "secular" features of the religion by admitting that the other-worldly soteriology of Buddhism belongs to its ideal of "ultimate concerns" yet that Buddhism also ministers to more immediate and pragmatical concerns. Ames (1964b:25) admitted that, although "Sinhalese Buddhism has only one way to salvation" - which is "redemption through systematic meditation" - it is apparent, nevertheless, that "not all Sinhalese Buddhists pursue this path." For these, "other goals of Buddhism must also be recognized."

Ames' interpretation of the religion of Ceylon's Buddhists implies that it either comprises several Buddhisms or else is a unified polylithic Buddhist religious system. Ames (1964b:40-41) admitted that "Sinhalese Buddhism" can be "divided into sophisticate and popular, or literati and folk levels of participation" having respectively different soteriological goals, and that "the sophisticate" - that is, the Buddhist monks, scholars, and intellectuals- "concentrates on the ascetic ideal of bhavanaya" while the peasant-folk attend to "merit-making (pinkama) for the reduction of suffering.[17] These distinctive soteriological goals indicate at least two Buddhisms serving respectively the higher and the lower strata of the Sinhalese society. The first corresponds to the "Great Tradition" and the second to "Little Tradition" in Sinhalese Buddhism. These may be perceived as two historic "levels", "expressions", or "forms" of the one historic tradition as it became shaped by the respective religious needs and purposes of the different strata of the Sinhalese Buddhist community.

These Buddhisms, therefore, are historically related to Theravāda Buddhism although Ames only assumed that the upper-level Buddhism leaned closer to the "Great Tradition" than did the folk-level Buddhism. His lack of expositional comment on this connection, however, reflects his minimal interest in Theravāda Buddhism in Sinhalese history and in the Sinhalese socio-culture. Ames (1964b.21 and 32) only made two passing-references to "Theravāda Buddhists"; and he stopped short of identifying the religion of the Sinhalese as "Buddhism." Instead, he supposed that "Sinhalese religion" and "Sinhalese Buddhism" are non-identical, and that "Sinhalese Religion" is a larger historical reality than "Sinhalese Buddhism." "Sinhalese religion" contains "Buddhist" components; but, the larger part of it is "non-Buddhist" even when "Magical-Animism" is dissociated from it.

For his systematic characterization of the total Sinhalese religious system, Ames (1964b.28) assumed that, like any polity or economy, a religious system comprises analytically distinguishable "units" or "subsystems". Each of the subsystems, moreover, serves "special functions for the total system" according to "a Durkheimian division of labor." The subsystems which serve "sacred functions" by upholding "other-worldly ideals" are "religious." The subsystems which serve "this-worldly ends" or "more directly contend with the world" are "profane" or not sacred; nor are they recognized as "sacred" by the people. These "profane" subsystems, accordingly, cannot be regarded as "religious components" of the "Sinhalese religion."

On the place of Buddhism within "the religion" of the Sinhalese, Ames recognized it as only "the first" among its component "religious subsystems." Yet he also concluded that this Buddhism is not integral to the "Sinhalese religion" since it is "largely set apart from ordinary affairs of the world." Nevertheless, even the secondary component subsystems, which reflect worldly concerns lack the "full legitimacy" of "religion" accorded by "Buddhist values." This is particularly so of two component subsystems which are closely associated with Buddhism but are not fully legitimated by it, namely, "the temple estate" and the "Buddhist nation-state."

A crucial feature of Ames' characterization of the Sinhalese religion is its relation to "Magical-animism." In his view, "Magical-animism" is not "religion," nor is it regarded by the Sinhalese as "religion." He reported that his informants judged it as being "absolutely profane (laukika) and altogether separate from Buddhism." Yet he also admitted that even if the Sinhalese "do not confuse Buddhism with magical animism" intellectually, nevertheless "in practice they frequently fuse them." It is this pragmatical fusion, moreover, which has led some scientific observers to adopt such "incorrect views" as that Sinhalese Buddhism is "contaminated by magic," or that "magic" is an intrinsic feature of Sinhalese Buddhism, or that "Buddhism forms the literate, sophisticate, Great Tradition part of [the] religion while the magic cults represent the folk, village, Little Tradition," or that Buddhism provides the outer "veneer" of the religion and the spirit-cults supply its "animistic substratum."

These observations, and Ames' response, indicate that they confused conceptual with empirical differentiations. Moreover, the intellectually compartmentalized distinctions which Ames' scholarly informants had made between the "sophisticate" and "unsophisticate" Sinhalese religion appeared effectively repudiated whenever they and other Sinhalese Buddhists in their communities practice their religion.[1] One is bound, therefore, to view circumspectly any representation of the Sinhalese religion which does not counter-balance the abstract intellectualistic compartmentalization of "Buddhist" and "non-Buddhist" components by the Sinhalese pragmatical syntheses of them. This includes an integral view of the contention by Ames (1964:40-46) that, although "the majority of [Sinhalese] Buddhists participate in spirit-propitiating and healing-magic animistic rites," they do not confuse their "popular form of Buddhism" with "magical-animism." It requires adopting a syncretic Buddhistic view of the Sinhalese religion despite Ames' observation that while the popular and sophisticate forms of Buddhism which "are sacred and highly systematized" have "different types of ritual bases" directed respectively toward "meditation" and "merit-making," their magical-animism is "profane or non-meritorious, relatively unsystematized, and stands outside these two Buddhist categories" even while it "caters to both types of Buddhists."

A similar syncretic view is needed against Ames' explanation of the two other "non-religious systems"- "the temple-estate" and the Buddhist theocratic (cakkavatti) "nation-state." Ames recognized their supportive function for the sophisticate Buddhism, because they provide economic and political "linkages" for "the regional and national [Buddhist] social institutions of monarchy, monastic landlordism, caste (jatiya), the service tenure system (rajakariya) and secular estates (nindagama)." But he also perceived the two systems as components of "a general societal economic complex" which is <u>non-religious</u> even though they are "directly related" to religion inasmuch as "it is in the estate and state systems especially, that Sinhalese religion articulates closely with secular institutions."

These compartmentalizations, however, are highly problematic for a scientific understanding of the religion of Ceylon's Theravāda Buddhists. Ames' restrictions of "Buddhism" and "Theravāda Buddhism" to an accidental adjunctive position vis-a-vis the total Sinhalese religious system which effectively denies the Buddhist identity and character of the larger remainder, are profoundly questionable. In this connection, Ames never followed through on his early statements (1964b:21 and 32) that those Sinhalese who do not exclusively espouse Hinduism, Islam, or Christianity "are Theravāda Buddhists" who espouse a religion which permits them to "indulge in a rich array of magical-animistic and other 'non-Buddhist' practices." This can only imply that the religion of Ceylon's "Theravāda Buddhists" is a syncretic form of <u>Theravāda Buddhism</u> in which are absorbed and harmonized the "rich array" of Buddhist and aboriginal, pre-Buddhist religious, magical and animistic beliefs and practices. Even if this complex system could not be called "Theravāda Buddhism" in the normative sense, it is "Theravāda Buddhism" in the historical sense of being the one religion traditionally espoused by the majority of Ceylon's "Theravāda Buddhists."

An anticipation of this wholistic viewpoint can be recognized in Ames' admission that there is no simple dichotomy in the Sinhalese religion between the Theravāda Buddhist "Great Tradition" and the "Little Tradition" of "Merit-making Buddhism" because these "sophisticate" and "popular" expressions of the Sinhalese religion appear simultaneously connected with each and every component and stratum of its totality. It appears, also, that Ames' compartmentalized empirical differentiations contradicted his syncretical observations on the symbiotic interrelation of the religion of the monks and the religion of the laity in Sinhalese Buddhism. The reverential etiquette practiced by the laity toward the monks is the other side of the reverential ministrations of ritual and educational services provided by the monks to the laity. Even the deity-temples (devalaya) which Ames contrasted with the Buddha-shrines (buddhalaya) as symbols of two contrary traditions have a manifest spacial integrality arising from the proximity of the locations of the temples and the shrines in monastic compounds. Inasmuch as the overall plan of the monastic compounds appears to mirror the Buddhist cosmological scheme, the relational arrangement of the temples and the shrines indicates the integrality of the temple and shrine systems in the Sinhalese Buddhist religion. There are no separate central and peripheral parts, or no element, feature, or functioning system, which lacks the Buddhist identity, character, and ethos of the total religious complex.[18]

The cosmological geography of the Buddhist monastery-temple precincts, providing the intimate locations of the altars, shrines, meditation-halls, etc. and of their "other-worldly" and "this-worldly" concerns and interests discredits Ames' denigratory explanation of the connections as a monkish device for "bringing magic under the control of the monks" and "the spirits under the suzerainty of Buddha." The interconnectional arrangement of the deity-temples and the Buddha-shrines under the one roof of the monastic complex affirms the

mutuality of the world-affirming and the world-denying
theisms, the one serving the needs of Buddhists seeking
the blessings and favours of the Buddha and his divine
and spirit agents, and the other serving the aspirations
of Buddhists seeking to glorify the Buddha and to
realize meditative union with his ideal Being.

These spacial locations and functional
interrelations of the systems also visually indicate
their "Buddhist" character and repudiate the scholar's
non-Buddhist definitional distinctions. Even the
distinctions behind Ames' structuralization of the
"magic-ritual" of the deity-shrines in an ascending
order of "levels" of "ritual purity" in ritual-objects
support the Buddhist identification. One should expect
that the materially grosser ritual offerings would be
made to the lower and the lowest nature-spirits (yakas
and pretayas) in the Buddhist pantheon, and that
offerings of "mixed" material-value would be appropriate
for planetary deities (graha-deviyas) at the next upper
level of ritual importance, and that the purest
offerings of gold, silver, and precious stones would be
reserved for the superior and higher deities around the
Buddha and his heavenly court. Moreover, the division
of labour which has the higher and the lower orders of
Buddhist monks and "priests" making the higher and lower
ritual-venerations harmonizes the ideal and the natural
concerns, needs, and aspirations of the Sinhalese
Buddhists.

On the other hand, since the lower orders of
spirits and deities have been mythologically
transmutable into higher orders of divine beings and the
converse also possible, so also rituals primarily
connected with Buddha-invocation serving "other worldly"
ends have been transmuted into magical-potencies

efficiently serving "this-worldly" objectives. In this light, Ames' contention (1964b:36) is unacceptable, that "Buddhist ritual . . . though possessing magical potency, is not magic" because it is "sacred" and not "profane," or that Buddhist ritual "competes" with the system of magic ritual or else does not compete since its healing power and other life-enhancing energies are only "secondary" to its "primary" function of "mental and spiritual development" which cannot be activated through magical rites.[19] For these primary and secondary functions are previously decided by the worshippers whenever they resort to and engage the ritual specialists either for pragmatical purposes in their daily life or occasionally for purely worshipful purposes directed to the Buddha.

In the final reckoning, it appears that Ames' highly sophisticated characterization of the Sinhalese religious system generally misrepresented the Sinhalese version of Theravāda Buddhism primarily because he transposed conceptual differentiations into empirical realities. Having adopted the Redfield-Marriott dichotomy for drawing systemic distinctions between Theravāda Buddhism Sinhalese Religion and Magical-animism, he used the answers of his informants for imputing these distinctions to the general religious understanding of Sinhalese Theravāda Buddhists. Nevertheless, while the architectonic rigidity and unhistorical character of his totalistic schematization of the religion prevented wholehearted acceptance by his contemporaries, it provided a model for later systematic studies and improved representations of Theravāda Buddhism, notably by Spiro, Tambiah, and Bechert.

E. Politicized Theistic Theravāda in Urban Śrī Laṅkā

The primary focus of socio-anthropological interest in religions of South and Southeast Asia from the nineteen-sixties was on the beliefs, practices, and traditions of the rural peasant-folk following Obeyesekere's remark that the "little communities" and their peasant-folk cultures are the proper concerns of anthropologists. Nevertheless, substantial studies of the urban contexts of the traditional religions were also undertaken along the lines of Milton Singer's explorations of the Sanskritic-Hindu socio-culture in contemporary urban India. These urban studies significantly advanced the socio-historical study of Buddhism and tested the applicability of Redfield's socio-cultural paradigm for the scientific interpretation and explanation of "popular religion" in rural and urban South and Southeast Asia.[20]

Important representative studies of urban Buddhism in South Asia which were published during the nineteen-sixties and seventies include researches by Hans-Dieter Evers (1968, 1972, 1977-78) and Heinz Bechert (1978). Although Bechert followed the profession of an Indologist or Buddhologist, he prefaced his historical studies of Buddhism in South and Southeast Asia with socio-scientific information on its present-day conditions. In the distinctive studies of Sinhalese religion which Evers published in 1968 and 1978, he primarily focussed on the "royal Buddhism" of Ceylon viewed against the historical backdrop of the medieval royal temple near Laṅkātilaka in Ceylon which he interpreted as an illustration of developmental processes behind the present complexity of Sinhalese Buddhism. His work, moreover, represents a transitional phase in the interpretive applications of the Redfield-

Marriott dichotomy to the religions of Buddhist South
Asia inasmuch as his earlier and later studies of the
"royal Buddhism" of medieval Śrī Laṅkā show the contrast
between the strong "Great Tradition/Little Tradition"
duality of his earlier work and the near abandonment of
the dichotomy in his later work. The explicit "urban"
emphasis appeared prominently in Monks, Priests and
Peasants: A Study of Buddhism and Social Structure in
Central Ceylon (1972). Its focus is urban rather than
rural, "sophisticate" rather than "peasant", and
"traditional" rather than "modern". It also reflects
the middle-phase of his socio-anthropology of Sinhalese
religion because it shows a methodological shift from
the "structural-functional approach" preferred by
anthropologists toward the start of the two-decade
period, and a new approach which Evers (1977-8;183-184)
referred to as the "cultural value approach." He
explained this as a "synchronic approach" combining
structuralist and politico-economic-historical
approaches to "religious structures in Śrī Laṅkā."

Evers (1972:99 and 177-8:183-5) drew from his
scientific approach his representation of the religion
of medieval urban Ceylon as a triple-component
metasystem comprising "Buddhism, Brāhmanism, and Hindu
Theism or Supernaturalism. He supposed that each
religion provides distinctive and contrasting values and
"functionally specific services" to the Sinhalese
society. He also supposed that by ascertaining which is
properly designated an historic expression of the
Buddhist "Great Tradition", and which is properly
perceived as a component of its "Little Tradition", the
interpretive viability of the Redfield-Marriott
dichotomy could be validated in the religious context of
Buddhist South Asia through a scientifically sound

representation of Sinhalese religion as a complex, historic, socio-cultural fact.

Evers' earlier work in 1968, however, reflects an uncritically enthusiastic use of Redfield's socio-cultural paradigm as it had been developed by Marriott. While his conclusions corresponded fairly closely to those of Obeyesekere and Ames in the early nineteen-sixties, they also indicate an improvement in regard to the observation that "when looking at the religion of Theravāda Buddhists as a whole . . . canonical Buddhism appears as only one aspect of the religion of Theravāda Buddhist societies." But this is still one step short of recognizing the whole complex as the religion of Theravāda Buddhism" demanding a rejection of the narrowly exclusivist use of the "label" solely for the "canonical" tradition.

But Evers did move toward the broader view of Theravāda Buddhism as a multifaceted religious system through his rejection of "the opinion perpetuated by generations of indologists" using arbitrarily abstracted scriptural references that "Buddhism is a philosophical or religious system of thought alone." On the other hand, his failure to follow up this observation toward an wholistic view reflects the pre-delimiting influence of those "indologists" upon his conception of Theravāda Buddhism and suppositions that "Theravāda Buddhism" is ideologically present in the Sinhalese religion but is not the defining feature of the religion as a whole. Instead, he thought of Theravāda Buddhism as an "incomplete" religion whose functional completeness required supplementations by non-Theravāda systems.[21]

Evers' representation of Theravāda Buddhism as "an incomplete religion" generated immediate and strong reactions from Theravāda Buddhist intellectuals and scholars. This is apparent in the lively correspondence on the matter during 1977 and 1978 between Evers and Seneviratne. Seneviratne (1977:381-382) also independently raised the issue of whether the "incompleteness" of Theravāda Buddhism is an empirical feature of it, or is a conceptualistic imputation following its abstraction from the historic religion of Buddhist South Asia's Theravāda Buddhist majority-population. Seneviratne rejected outright the notion of an "incomplete" Theravāda Buddhist religion, and also Evers' conclusion (1968:549) that "it has been demonstrated that Theravāda Buddhism does not exist by itself, but has its counterpart in the form of other systems of belief."[22]

Nevertheless, it was the manifest religious pluralism in the Sinhalese socio-culture that led Evers into his distinctive scientific interpretation and explanation of "the social organization of the Sinhalese religion" in terms of its diverse component "value-systems" and their structural-functional and historical relationships. In "Buddha and the Seven Gods" (1968:549), he argued that viewing "the religion of Theravāda Buddhists as a whole" discloses its Theravāda Buddhist value-system as only one of its components. In it "there exist two religious systems side by side, which are kept clearly apart in theory and [in practice by being] served by different religious specialists, but are used by the laity simultaneously, and . . . viewed by them as complementary and interdependent." The two coinciding religious systems are "the Buddhist system . . . supplemented by the system of the gods."[23]

Evers proceeded from this duality toward the supposition of a third historically-distinct religious system based on the conception of divine kingship. The emphatic finality of his pluralistic view of the religion espoused by the Sinhalese is also notable for its unique presuppositions. Firstly, it clearly gives the precedence to Sinhalese "Buddhism" not on historical grounds relating to the general history of the Sinhalese socio-culture, but on empirical grounds of the de facto prominence of Buddhism in Sinhalese life and society. Secondly, it denies, by implication, that there was ever any syncretistic fusion and absorption-into-each-other of these distinctive and conceptually isolable religious systems. Yet in his later correspondence with Seneviratne (1977-8:183-185) he amplified an earlier statement made in "Buddha and the Seven Gods" by contending that "Sinhalese Religion" is an wholistic synthesis of conceptually distinguishable yet functionally interrelated "Buddhist" and "non-Buddhist" systems; "Sinhalese Buddhism" is a "triple system" formed by the vihare-system of Buddha-worship, the devale-system of worship of the gods, and "a palace system" based upon, and ritually expressed through, a conception of divinized kingship; and these systems are distinguishable by their "contrasting values" and their "functionally specific services . . . to the society."

The relation of "Theravāda Buddhism" to the total system of the Sinhalese religion is problematic in Evers' representation of the Sinhalese religious complexity. He connected it solely with the vihare-system of "Buddha-worship", that is, to only one of the three component-systems of "Sinhalese Buddhism". He does not appear to have been aware of the real implication behind this delimitation, that it denies the "Theravāda Buddhist" identity, character, and social reality of "the religion of the Theravāda Buddhists of Ceylon." The pervasive influence of Theravāda Buddhism upon all _three_ systems of the Sinhalese religion, and upon its suppositional "non-Buddhist" components, implies a "Theravāda" buddhaization of the total system in the sense that the _whole_ is the total expression of its parts. Evers should have perceived this pervasion of the total system by Theravāda Buddhism in the architecture and ritual organization of the central Buddhist shrine in the medieval royal temple near Laṅkātilaka. His finely detailed description, including its architectural ground plan, its documented ritual, and its economic and administrative organization, and overall explanation of the temple plan (1968:544) as being "built around a spacially and ritually closely integrated complex of the temples of the gods, the Buddha, and a palace for the king," and serving the annual, public, "gigantic rituals of identification of the Buddha, the Gods, and the government," makes a full sense only when the Theravāda Buddhist character of the total system is recognized due to its focus in the iconography and the ideology of the Buddha. But it is also evident in the traditional recognition of the totality as "Theravāda Buddhism" by Ceylon's Theravāda Buddhists.

The absence of such a conclusion is all the more surprising because Evers came so close to it. K.R. Norman (1976:468), who reviewed Evers' work (1972:98), commented that Evers "surprises himself with his conclusion that in the social order of Theravada Buddhism there are gods and demons, landlords and aristocrats, elaborate festivals and rituals." Yet, Evers did not carry through the implications of this plurality in regard to a polylithic, socially-stratified, complex Theravāda Buddhist religion. For in Norman's opinion, the supernaturalistic component in

Theravāda Buddhism "need surprise no one who has ever read anything written by Evers' fellow-sociologists" nor yet, on that matter, by anyone who has noticed the frequent mentionings of yakkhas and devas and rajaputtas in the earliest Buddhist texts. Norman also remarked in response to Evers' ideas on Theravāda Buddhism that if ever a "pure" form of it had existed, it must have been "very short lived." The corollary to this is that if, at any time, "Buddhism", "Brāhmanism", and Hindu Supernaturalism could have existed in competitive proximity to each other in mainland India, these nevertheless must have become fully integrated within Buddhism and Hinduism even centuries prior to their expansion beyond mainland India.

These syncretic mergences of the traditions prior to the introduction of Buddhism into Ceylon also preclude certain suppositions behind Evers' socio-historical study of "royal Buddhism" or "the palace system" focussed in the palace-temple of Lankātilaka in medieval Ceylon. K.R. Norman (1976:468) found fault with his interpretation both on empirical and historical grounds. He thought that Evers had failed to provide empirical supports for his contention that a "cult of the god-king," focussed on the concept of devaraja as an epithet of the god Śakra (Pali = Sakka), had historically existed as the heart of "the palace system" among the Kandyan aristocracy.[24] Nor did Evers' empirical data conclusively demonstrate that three historically distinctive religions corresponding to the worship of the Buddha, the worship of the deities, and the worship of the divinized king, were separately introduced, independently functioned, and became subsequently fused into the Buddhism of Ceylon centuries after its introduction into Śrī Lankā. Nevertheless,

Evers' sophisticated exposition of the economic and the political dimensions of the early and the medieval Buddhist systems of urban Ceylon contributed significantly to socio-historical knowledge on Theravāda Buddhism. In particular, his stated purpose (1977-8:185) of setting the Sinhalese Theravāda Buddhist system within "the macro-sociological context of the social and economic history of Śrī Laṅka" was germinative of ideas for other scholars - such as Nur Yalman and Heinz Bechert - who built upon his work.

Bechert's scholarship on Theravāda Buddhism is especially important because, for nearly two decades between the publication of his major study of Buddhism and society titled Buddhismus, Staat und Gesellschaft in den Ländern Theravāda Buddhismus (1966) and "Contradictions in Sinhalese Buddhism" (1973, 1978), his work has led the fields of history and sociology of Theravāda Buddhism. Hence, any critique of the historical presuppositions, the methodological assumptions, and the interpretational conclusions in his work will have crucial bearings upon our modern knowledge of Theravāda Buddhism in South and Southeast Asia. His work is especially significant inasmuch as it lends considerable credibility to a modern pluralistic view of Theravāda Buddhism in regard to its canonical and non-canonical formations, its philosophical, theistic, cultic, and magical features and expressions, its local, parochial, regional, and universal historic actualizations, and its "traditional" and its "modern" conditions. His Indological and Buddhological perspectives on Theravāda Buddhist history are uniquely informed by Redfieldian methodological and interpretational considerations. Indeed, his penchant for prefacing his academic-historical approach to the

Theravāda tradition by socio-anthropological insights on
its contemporary expressions may have justified the
inclusion of Bechert's name in the list of citations
made by K.R. Norman (1976:468) on "the sociological
perspectives" in studies of the Sinhalese "Theravāda
Buddhist Sangha."[25]

Norman's citation of Bechert in a critique of
Evers' work reflect the complementarity of their socio-
anthropological and academic-historical research on
urban Sinhalese Theravāda Buddhism particularly in
regard to the interconnections of Buddhist religion with
national polity during Buddhism's medieval and modern
periods. Yet Norman also showed that Bechert's
exposition of the relationship of Sinhalese Buddhism and
national polity is no less sophisticated than S.J.
Tambiah's monumental study of Thai Buddhism and national
polity. But Bechert's sociological orientation toward
the history of Theravāda Buddhism is fully apparent in
"Theravāda Buddhist Sangha: Some General Observations
on Historical and Political Factors in its Development"
(1970:761ff.). There, Bechert presented an introductory
preface on Max Weber's analytical approach to the
history of the Sangha. Moreover, this Weberian
sociological backdrop of his major historical study of
Theravāda Buddhism indicates the sources of a
sociological interest in Theravāda Buddhism which
flowered in his later work.

In "Einige Fragen der Religionssoziologie und
Structur des suedasiatischen Buddhismus," which appeared
in the International Yearbook for the Sociology of
Religion 4 (1968:251-253), Bechert made "a detailed
discussion of Weber's opinions." He intentionally
followed up on this discussion in his 1970 essay which
is also significant in the context of Redfieldian

studies of Buddhism during the nineteen-sixties and seventies because Bechert (1963:139-153) had already become impressed by Obeyesekere's socio-anthropological approach to the Sinhalese religion. Later, however, Bechert (1972:774, n.43) found untenable Obeyesekere's sharply dualistic "definition of Great Tradition and Little Tradition in Theravāda countries" although he appears to have held fewer reservations about the dualistic Redfieldian representations of the religion by Ames (1964a:21-52), Evers (1968:241-250), and D.E. Smith (1965 and 1966).

Bechert (1970:774f.) did not restrict his interest in Theravāda Buddhism and Saṅghika politics to its Sinhalese historical backdrop but extended this to Burma also in the broader context of "the religious background of the Theravāda Buddhist countries" and of the history of the Theravāda Buddhist Saṅgha. His reason for focussing on the social organization of the Saṅgha seems to have been that it could be perceived as a model for the total social organization of Theravāda Buddhism in Buddhist South Asia, as well as the most significant informational source on the historical backdrop of modern Theravāda Buddhism and on "the religious factors" behind "the political and social upheaval in the Buddhist countries of South and Southeast Asia in the recent past."

Bechert (1970:774), accordingly, set the sociological parameters of his exposition of Theravāda Buddhism as the contexts of "the general political and social situation" of the Theravāda Buddhist countries of contemporary Southeast Asia. He proposed to contrast "canonical Buddhism" with "popular religion," and in regard to the "popular religion," to ascertain "the basic differences of the popular religions" in "the

several countries of Theravāda Buddhism," and to explain
the interrelations of "popular Buddhism" - that is, the
"religious practices" of the peasant-folk which are
based on the so-called 'Great Tradition' of 'literary
Buddhism' - with "the non-Buddhist popular cults of the
so-called 'Little Tradition' religion."[26]

Yet the promising outcome of his distinctions
between the formal dimensions and distinctive features
of the canonical and the popular forms of Buddhism
proved disappointingly problematic in several respects.
His expositions do not indicate clearly the character of
the "religion" in the principal Theravāda Buddhist
countries, whether it comprises one, three, five, or
more distinctive "historic" traditions, or whether these
are conceptually envisaged components of a polylithic
Theravada Buddhist metasystem. They do indicate,
however, that, like his professional contemporaries, he
assumed that some of the features and component
subsystems are "non-Buddhist traditions," but differed
from them by his eclectic observation (1970:775) that:
"Buddhism has always been in actual manifestation . . .
an integrated religious system including popular
beliefs."

Bechert apparently was caught in the same
Redfieldian net which conceptually separated the
Buddhist "Great Tradition" - enshrined in the Buddhist
sacred texts and serving as the normative ideal and
authoritative source of Buddhist values - from the
"Little Tradition" comprising both "the religious
practices of the peasant population based on the so-
called 'Great Tradition' of literary Buddhism but not in
full agreement with the real understanding of the ideas
incorporated," and the functionally complementary system
of "the non-Buddhist popular cults."[27] This

conceptualistized differentiation agreed with Obeyesekere's representation of the Sinhalese religion as the "canonical Buddhism" - which "is practically the same in the five Theravāda Buddhist countries"- complemented both by "popular Buddhism" which "shows similarities only" with the canonical Buddhism, and by "the non-Buddhist popular cults" which are "entirely different in Ceylon, Burma, and Thailand." But he added to the conceptualistic differentiation his eclectic historical explanation in which he observed Buddhism never functioned in South Asia "as a purely religious theory" since "only in its actual manifestation as an integrated religious system including popular beliefs" could "Buddhism have influenced political and social developments."

This indicates Bechert's adoption of current sociological distinctions between canonical and historical Theravāda Buddhism without deciding which is properly the subject of a "history" of Theravāda Buddhism in South and Southeast Asia: the conceptualistically abstracted "canonical Buddhism" drawn from the Pali scriptural canon or the total social fact of the religion of South and Southeast Asia's Theravāda Buddhist majority. Moreover, while his primary interest in the political factors behind the historical development of the Saṅgha amplified significant details on the historical actualization of a "real" or "historic" Theravāda Buddhist religion in South Asia, these were not extensive enough to incorporate "the history" of its "popular" traditional expressions also. He assumed only that the historical development of the Saṅgha was the major feature of the historical development of Theravāda Buddhism in South Asia. He made this observation precisely at the point in his 1970 essay (p. 775) where he began to broaden his analysis of "the Buddhism of the Theravāda countries" through unfortunately vague differentiations of its component subsystems and "religious institutions," principally "the Saṅgha," "the state cults," the "cults of the gods," and "magical rites."

In "Contradictions in Sinhalese Buddhism" (1973, 1978), Bechert reiterated the central hypothesis which he had originally presented in Buddhismus, Staat und Gesellschaft (1966) and had assumed to be "demanded" by the arrangement of the extant documentary material on the development of "political Buddhism" in Ceylon. It was that the principal characteristic of "modern Buddhism" - as shown by its reform movements - is "an effort to return to the sources" and "to bring about a real generation of original conditions." This recollective "effort" toward contemporizing conditions of the ancient past causes "tension" between "the still-effective forces of traditional Buddhism, with its ties to historical social conditions, legal relationships and manners of thinking" of "Buddhists" on the one hand, and "the determined reformers" trying to change the tradition to suit "modern" social and cultural conditions on the other. These "tensions" in turn cause confusions over the meaning of Buddhism both for Buddhists themselves and also for scholars attempting to provide scientific explanations of traditional Buddhism's contemporary manifestations. "Modernists" and "traditionalists" can resolve the tensions and reduce the interpretational ambiguities, by adopting "an historical viewpoint" on "the meaning of Buddhism." But he meant by this adopting historical explanations of Theravāda Buddhism's ancient past current among academic historians and Buddhologists.

Bechert referred to Hermann Oldenberg's "classic Buddha book" as support for his opinion that early Buddhism was the religion of "an elite community" and not a "Sanghika version" of a more generalized "popular" or "lay" Buddhism. He noted Oldenburg's crucial contention that this "pure" Buddhism of the monastic elite did not come about because "there was no place for the laity in early Buddhism," but because a clear and specific lay-version of early Buddhism "had not yet developed." He also built upon Oldenberg's historical distinctions additional historical conclusions about a primal elitist or intellectualized Buddhism, a later yet temporally-proximate "monastic" Buddhism, and a still later "lay Buddhism" having originated within and developed during the early period of Indian Buddhism.

Bechert's historical assumptions about Buddhism in India accordingly stand or fall upon the validity of Oldenburg's assumptions about the socio-cultural conditions of the growth of Buddhism in ancient India. Oldenburg's elitist viewpoint is apparently supportable from the monastic historiographical records. On the other hand, the earliest Buddha-biographies clearly indicate a strong lay-element in the early organization and four "orders" of the Buddhist Sangha. Moreover, it could be plausibly argued that the contemporary Brahmanism prevented a distinctive "lay-Buddhism" from arising contemporaneously with the monastic Buddhism inasmuch as the original lay-adherents of Buddhism and the majority of Sanghika members did not abandon their brahmanical tradition, neither its rites and rituals, its festivals and customs, its supernaturalistic superstructure and animistic substratum, nor its other religious frameworks which shaped their brahmanical understanding of the Buddha's person and teaching. Even the inner circle of the Buddha's disciples drew their interpretational structures for Buddhism from their traditional brahmanical heritage. This heritage, moreover, must have had a moulding influence upon every form of Buddhism prior to its emergence as a distinctive religious system and social institution of Aśokan India.

Despite the paucity of empirical evidence on the immediate impact of the brahmanical tradition on the formative shaping of early monastic and lay Buddhism, sufficient knowledge of the brahmanic socio-culture is available from its textual tradition for reconstructing the brahmanical conditions, forces and processes which must have shaped early Buddhism. Even the forms of present-day popular Buddhism identified by Michael Ames as the "pinkama Buddhism" of Ceylon and by Melford E. Spiro as the "kammatic Buddhism" of Burma, present animistic and supernaturalistic features similar to those which the laity of ancient brahmanical India could have brought into their "lay" Buddhism according to its representations in the surviving monuments of early Buddhist architecture, sculpture, and art.

Bechert, however, was able to withhold "an historical viewpoint" on this lay-Buddhism inasmuch as it was not important for his reconstruction of the processes of politicization in early Indian Theravāda Buddhism. He found ample information on those processes in Oldenburg's "classic history" of early Buddhism for his own socio-historical study of Buddhism and national polity in Buddhismus, Staat und Gesellschaft. He perceived that the success of Aśoka's "Buddhist mission" to Ceylon, and those of his successors, depended on how well those missions served the political and economic interests of Sinhalese rulers. These interests, in turn, shaped the political form of Sinhalese Buddhism through "an extensive identification" of Sanghika, national, and public interests supported by the "public roles" of Buddhist monks serving those interests.

Bechert recognized this politicized Sinhalese Buddhism as a componentially complex metasystem comprising diverse "Buddhist" and "non-Buddhist" subsystems. Bechert (1978:192-197) attempted an integral wholistic representation of the Sinhalese political Buddhist metasystem in terms of the conjunctions of historically different religions, of Buddhism and the aboriginal "cult of the gods" and the "cults of Hindu origin." He also contrasted this Buddhism with the "canonical Theravāda Buddhism," and distinguished the latter from the theistic and cultic Buddhism of the laity. He advanced the modern sociological understanding of the lay-Buddhism by rejecting the current supposition that it had historically developed through an assimilation of a "Hindu tradition" into the Sinhalese religion without any prior buddhaization of the Hindu tradition. He also distinctively elucidated the popularizational mechanisms of the laicized Buddhism by showing how the formal and static Buddhism of the Sinhalese Saṅgha became "embroiled" in the day-to-day secular, political, schismatic, and sectarian concerns of the Sinhalese society from early to modern times, and how the Buddhism became syncretically diversified into the popular Buddhist cult where "the worthlessness of cult activities as taught by the Buddha was silently ignored, . . . cultic activities of the most varied kind were built in as merit," and the whole transformed into a complex system of merit-making theory and practice.

Bechert also apparently expanded Evers' conception of Theravāda Buddhism as an "incomplete religion" by finding that incompleteness in Sinhalese Buddhism, in the god-cults, and in their counterparts in the other Theravāda countries of Southeast Asia. But this contradicted his observation that, outside of Ceylon, "Buddhism has integrated itself with the cults." Moreover, this notion of Sinhalese Buddhism's "incompleteness" prevented a wholistic view of the Sinhalese religion incorporating its "canonical" Buddhist, its regional or national Buddhist, and its cultic expressions among the upper, middle, and lower levels of the Sinhalese Buddhist society even though he had found an historical instance of such a stratificational complexity in Theravāda Buddhism within "the Buddhist group of Baruas in East Bengal" in whose Theravāda Buddhist religion the buddhaization of local pre-Buddhist cults had long been institutionally incorporated.[28]

On the whole, however, Bechert's analytical study of Theravāda Buddhism exposed to view the six principal components comprising the religion of South and Southeast Asia's Buddhist populations. These are: (i) "a monastic Buddhism of the Theravāda type"; (ii) "the Great Tradition canonical or literary Buddhism"; (iii) "popular Buddhism" having a foundation of localized "Great Tradition Buddhist elements" supplemented by "a cult of the gods" and "magical rites"; (iv) non-Buddhist "cults of the gods"; (v) "court Buddhism" or state-religion composed of a buddhaized version of a regional vaiṣṇavite-brāhmanism; and (vi) a modern, politicized and "resurgent Buddhism" or "modern Theravāda Buddhism." This last component is not "identical with" the "canonical Buddhism" although it is part of the continuity of the historical tradition from early to modern times.[29]

Through these distinctions, Bechert indicated the complexity of Sinhalese Buddhism more clearly and systematically than his contemporaries and predecessors. His componential differentiation of the Sinhalese religion also confronted sociologists and historians interested in Theravāda Buddhism with the new historical question of how it could have come about, and particularly how the imported Buddhist components and the aboriginal "non-Buddhist" components had become integrated. He also indicated the interpretational refinements to which the componential differentiations are amenable around the problem of their connection and identity with Theravāda Buddhism, including whether or not the "Theravāda" label is properly attachable to any of them.

Bechert's analysis leaves several options open. The "Theravāda" label could be entirely deleted and each of the components identified respectively as "canonical Buddhism," "monastic Buddhism," "popular Buddhism," "state Buddhism," and so on. Alternatively, the labels "Buddhist" and "Buddhism" could be deleted following the example of Terwiel (1976:391) who preferred making reference to "religion in Theravāda Buddhist countries" without assuming its Buddhist or non-Buddhist identity.[30] On the other hand, the "Theravāda" label could be attached to any component subsystem of a national religion of Buddhist South Asia which displays features and elements identifiable with Theravāda Buddhism in the Pali Buddhist canonical and historiographical literature. Conversely, the "Theravāda" label could be applied to any aboriginal and indigenous religious system of Buddhist South Asia which has become assimilated through buddhaization into the Theravāda Buddhist tradition. Or, lastly, the

"Theravāda" label could be reserved solely for the canonical Buddhist tradition espoused by members of the Theravāda Buddhist Sangha and Theravāda Buddhist scholars and intellectuals in Buddhist South Asia.

The socio-anthropological research on religions in Buddhist South Asia during the nineteen-sixties and seventies indicates that the majority of scientists using the Redfield-Marriott dichotomy adopted the second of these options. By coining the terms "Sinhalese religion," "Burmese religion," and "Thai religion" for "the religion" of each of these Theravāda Buddhist countries, they were free to ascertain or determine which of the component systems could appropriately be labelled as "Buddhist" or as "non-Buddhist" prior to the syncretic fusion of the "Buddhist" and "pre-Buddhist" systems into the national Buddhist complexes and the successive transformations through which this syncretic Buddhist complex historically passed in South Asia. Nevertheless, the decision to apply the "Theravāda" label either to any part or to the totality of a national religious complex raises crucial historical as well as definitional questions about the character and development of Theravāda Buddhism in Ceylon and other Theravāda countries of Southeast Asia. Yet the answers to those questions could only remain tentative and speculative without an empirically-grounded consensus on which of the definitional and interpretational alternatives behind the various options provide the best fit for the socio-historical explanation of Theravada Buddhism in South and Southeast Asia.

Bechert did not decide an option. Nevertheless, he made an outstanding contribution toward a pluralistic conception of Theravāda Buddhism in Ceylon and the rest of Buddhist South Asia. His multi-componential, structural-functional characterization of the total system was built upon foundations in Michael Ames' systematic representation of the religion. He rounded off the nineteen-seventies with a scientifically advanced understanding of the character and history of the complex religion espoused by Ceylon's majority of Theravada Buddhists without certainly establishing the "Theravada" identity of the whole. In his analysis of its componential complexity, he indicated clearly: its "monastic Buddhism of the Theravāda type," its "Great Tradition canonical or literary Buddhism," its "popular Buddhism" component comprising "Great Tradition" Theravāda elements; its buddhaized "vaiṣṇavite-brāhmanic" or "state-Buddhism" component, its "resurgent Buddhist" or recently modernized and politicized Buddhism component, and is Buddhist and buddhaized "cultic" and animistic features and elements. His interpretations of the system tackled head-on the "definitional ambiguities" and "confusions" bedeviling the understanding by "traditionalists" and "modernists" concerning the relation of "modern" Buddhism to the Theravāda tradition by indicating the need for "an historical viewpoint" which could link the present complexity of Buddhism in Srī Laṅka with its preceding historic phases. His historical viewpoint integrated the earlier with the later formations and developments of the political, economic, and other socio-cultural expressions of Theravāda Buddhism in Ceylon, and their meldings with Ceylon's ancient aboriginal religious systems, displaying thereby the vibrant syncretistic process which became "the history" of the Theravāda Buddhist religion of the Sinhalese people.

Chapter Three. Burmese Animism and Theravāda Buddism

Compared with sociological writing on religions in Ceylon and Thailand, fewer sociological studies of religion during the nineteen-sixties and seventies applied the Redfield-Marriott dichotomy to Buddhism in Burma. Concise histories of Burmese Buddhism did appear in cultural surveys of Burma and of Southeast Asia such as Georges Coedes' classic "history" published in 1962 and translated into English in 1966 by H.M. Wright as The Making of South East Asia. Several specialized religio-political histories of Burmese Buddhism were published during the nineteen-sixties and seventies, principally Emanuel Sarkisyanz' Buddhist Backgrounds of the Burmese Revolution (1965), Donald Eugene Smith's Religion and Politics in Burma (1965), and John Ferguson's edition of E. Michael Mendelson's Sangha and State in Burma: A Study of Monastic and Sectarian Leadership (1975). "The Advent of Buddhism to Burma" and its subsequent fusion of Vaiṣṇava, Mahāyāna, and Theravāda religious systems were the subjects of several sophisticated studies by G.H. Luce reviewed in Buddhist Studies in Honour of I.B. Horner, edited by L. Cousins in 1974. But among the principal sociological contributions of those decades to scientific knowledge on the folk-level of contemporary Burmese Theravāda Buddhism there are significant interpretational applications of the Redfield-Marriott dichotomy as to warrant this analytical study. The essay by John Brohm on "Buddhism and Animism in a Burmese Village" (1963), and two by Melford E. Spiro on Burmese Supernaturalism (1967) and on Buddhism and Society: A Great Tradition and its Burmese Vicissitudes (1970) are sufficiently representative of the interpretational strengths and weaknesses of the applications of Redfield's socio-cultural paradigm to Southeast Asian Buddhism.

A. The Animistic Character of Burmese Buddhism

John Brohm's study of animism in Burmese Buddhism
re-introduced a late nineteenth-century "thin veneer"
theory by portraying Burmese Buddhism as a type of
buddhaized animism. He noticed that the majority of the
Burmese who have animistic beliefs and practices
nevertheless recognize themselves as "Theravāda
Buddhists." This fact carries implications on the
character and history of Theravāda Buddhism in Burma.

Brohm's interpretation of Burmese Buddhism is
distinctive inasmuch as he eliminated the conceptual
distancing of the "Great Tradition" of Theravāda
Buddhism from the "Little Tradition" supernaturalism and
animism of the Theravāda Buddhist peasant-folk, and
"religion" from "magic" drawn so sharply for the
religion of the Sinhalese village-folk by Michael Ames
and for the religion of the Burmans by Melford E. Spiro.
Yet his interpretation of Burmese religious complexity
was pursued from the perspective of the Redfield-
Marriott dichotomy in its applications to "traditional"
religions in contemporary South and Southeast Asia.

Brohm adopted the current anthropological stance of
contemporary anthropologists giving priority in their
researches to the aboriginal religion of Burma's
village-dwelling majority of peasant folk. But unlike
the majority of his contemporaries, Brohm (1963:155)
denied any real duality between "animism" and
"Buddhism", but recognized instead the unity of the
religion of the Burmese peasant-folk formed by the
integration of their Animism and Supernaturalism with
Burma's Theravāda Buddhist tradition. In this respect,
his work contrasted the substantive richness of the folk
Theravāda Buddhism with the substantive paucity of the
conceptualized "canonical" Theravāda Buddhism espoused

by Burma's elites. He found the supernaturalistic and animistic superstructures and substructures of the popular Buddhism so prominent that their religion might have been labelled as either "animistic Theravāda Buddhism" or "Theravāda Buddhist animism."

Nevertheless, the current restricted use of the "Theravāda" label prevented an explicit declaration of this implication of the religion of Burma's peasant-majority of Theravāda Buddhists. Instead, he couched his anthropological interpretation of the Buddhism of Burma's peasant-folk in animistic terms, and used the terminology of "Great Tradition" and "Little Tradition" for portraying the syncretic relationship of the "Great Tradition" of Theravāda Buddhism with "the superstitions of the Little Tradition" which "fill the religious world" of the peasant-folk.

The "Great Tradition/Little Tradition" duality in Brohm's representation of the Burmese religion reflected the current scholarly distinctions which applied the concept of "Great Tradition" solely to the canonical tradition of Theravāda Buddhism, and the "Little Tradition" concept to the supernaturalistic and animistic practices of Burma's peasant folk. Brohm empirically recognized Burma's majority of peasant-folk as "Theravāda Buddhists," yet did not recognize their folk-religion as a popular form of "Theravāda Buddhism." At the most he allowed its recognition as a type of animistic-Buddhism or as a type of Buddhist-animism.

Even so, a crucial feature of Brohm's interpretational representation of the religion was his insistence on the integral unity of the religion in the sense that the Burmese could not be religiously characterized at any given moment as "half-animist" and "half-Buddhist." In other words, he admitted that the scholars' conceptual distinctions between "animism" and "Buddhism" are empirically transcended by the pragmatically unified animistic and Buddhist religion of Burma's Buddhist population. He attempted, accordingly, a definitional compromise. Their religion, he observed, is a distinctive "Burmese" type of Buddhist religion which is "not readily identified by references to scripture" although it has Buddhist scriptural and other elements conjoined also with non-Buddhist religious elements. It is, accordingly, an organic whole. But, it does not meet the current scholarly definition of Theravāda Buddhism. Therefore, for want of a currently available label, it may be called "Burmese religion" whose distinctive character lies in its animistic orientation and pragmatical complementarity with the canonical Theravāda Buddhism.

Brohm was not ready to call this religion of the peasant-folk "Animism" since, in his view, animism is not a "religion" but only the psychical orientation behind the system of magical rites which pragmatically complement their Buddhist rituals. But Brohm (1963:156 n.2) both explicitly disconnected animism from the religion of the Burmese, yet also relegated the system of animistic beliefs and rituals to "the residuum of non-canonical beliefs and behavior" in the religion of the Burmese. This necessarily implies recognition of an animistic component in the religion of the Burmese Buddhists, or, more generally, of the religion as an animistically-oriented folk-type of Buddhism. This implication in turn draws a definitional contrast between the Buddhist religion as it has been empirically observed and the normative definition of that Theravāda Buddhism by Buddhist textual-historians.

Instead of deciding which is empirically and historically sound and valid, Brohm relegated his empirical data to the new conceptual category of "Burmese religion" and justified its contrastive separation from "Theravāda Buddhism" on account of the "non-normative" features which are prominent in the religion of Burma's peasant-majority of Theravāda Buddhists. Even so, he did not overlook the assimilational proximity of the normative or canonical tradition and the folk-religion of the peasants. His field-data demanded an interpretation of the Burmese religion which did definitional justice to the integrality of the religion's normative and non-normative features and to the prestigious prominence of its "Buddhist" features. In short, the religious reality espoused by the majority of Burma's Theravāda Buddhists demanded a definitional characterization embracing the full range of its scripturalistic, its theistic, and its animistic elements, and its labelling either as "Animistic Theravāda Buddhism" or as "Theravāda Buddhist Supernaturalism."

As an anthropologist, Brohm did not have to decide upon one or the other of these plausible conclusions. As an anthropologist, he was primarily interested in the real and everyday religion of Burma's peasant population. This could be empirically disassociated from the normative of canonical Theravada Buddhism stored in the "refined corpus of written teachings conveying idealized values" and imposing no need of being "measured in terms of human behavior." Brohm (1963:157f.) accordingly set his parameters of anthropological inquiry into the Burmese religion within a threefold systematic procedure: firstly, for making "a series of generalizations" concerning the real

character of contemporary Burmese folk-religion;
secondly, providing a description of Burmese religious
behaviour "illustrative of these generalizations"; and
finally, focussing "these illustrations and
generalizations . . . upon the problem of terminology in
the discussion of Burmese religion" and religions of
neighbouring peoples in Thailand and Cambodia "many of
whom share some of the main patterns of Burmese
religion."[2]

Brohm believed that his descriptive generalizations
and illustrations would demonstrate the intricate
weavings of "Buddhist" and "non-Buddhist" elements in
the religion of the Burmese people. This demonstration
in turn would correct current misrepresentations of the
religion arising from "terminological confusion" and
mistaken attributions of empirical reality to conceptual
distinctions, and would disprove the assumption that the
history of Burmese religion can be transcribed as the
account of the confluences and divergences of two or
more religions principally distinguished as "Buddhism"
and "Animism." He supposed that his interpretational
approach would unequivocally endorse an empirically
grounded and historically valid account of the religion
of the Burmese which is not bedeviled by the
multiplication of systemic entities. He concluded that
"it is clearly non-descriptive of [the religious]
behavior [of the Burmese] for us to speak [of them] in
terms of animists or Buddhists - or of their religion,
even, as 'animism' and 'Buddhism,' since Buddhism as
practiced here is a form of animism" which reflects a
Buddhist concession to it along with a Buddhist
"scriptural toleration of a Hindu-based pantheon of
deities."[3]

Surprisingly, Brohm did not clinch this observation by admitting that Burmese Buddhism is Hinduistic and Animistic, or that it comprises the old aboriginal, pre-Buddhistic, animistic religion of the Burmese brought within the imported traditions of Indian Theravāda and Mahāyāna Buddhism. Instead, the ambiguity of his concluding statements leaves readers uncertain on whether or not he thought that the religion of Buddhist Burma's peasant-majority is indeed "Buddhist," or is specifically "Theravāda Buddhist," or is a form of "Animism," or is even something else for which only the new label of "Burmese religion" is appropriate.

B. Theravāda Buddhism and the Burmese Religion

However, a representation of Burmese "Theravāda Buddhism" did emerge in Brohm's work. It seems taht Brohm intended to provide a unitary definition of the Burmese religion on the empirical ground that there is "only one religion . . . practiced by the Burmese people about which we can legitimately speak. For want of an established term, we can call it Burmese religion." Yet he could not overlook its integral connections with Burma's historic Theravāda Buddhism. He recognized certain Theravāda Buddhist "scriptural referents of Burmese religion" as an "unquestionably . . . important element" of the general system of the Burmese religion" which could not be ocnfused with ritual and other practices in the "Burmese religious behaviour" which are also "traditional" but are "not necessarily scripturally derived." These indicate a substantive interconnection between Theravāda Buddhism and the Burmese religion. Yet apart from the Theravāda Buddhist scripturalist referents, Brohm observed that the Burmese religion appears to be substantially "non-Theravāda" and even "non-Buddhist in the normative sense."

But Brohm had to contend with the problematic fact of the impression made by Theravāda Buddhism upon the religion of Burma's Theravāda Buddhist peasants. If the scripturalist referents were merely supplementative additions from Theravāda Buddhism, then the Burmese religion could not be called "Theravāda Buddhism" in either a "normative" or an "historical" sense. But if the "Theravāda" component provided its defining characteristic, then the religion of Burma's peasant-majority of Theravāda Buddhists had to be viewed historically as a Burmese mode of the Theravāda Buddhist religion formed by a syncretic historical process of mergence and mutual absorption between the aboriginal, pre-Buddhist religion of Burma's peasant-folk and Indian Buddhism. Furthermore, instead of its fundamental "non-Buddhist" character, its "Buddhist" character had to be perceived as dominant.

The conditions and forces behind the syncretization of Theravāda Buddhism and Burma's aboriginal and indigenous religions comprise accordingly the historical factor behind the Theravāda Buddhist "religion" in Burma. Although Brohm did not focus special attention upon this historical factor, he nevertheless made references to it in the context of seeking "an alternative approach" to the Burmese religion which could circumvent or avoid the confusing dualistic stratifications and compartmentalizations currently reflecting in appropriate empiricalizations of the Redfield-Marriott dichotomy contrasting the "Great Tradition" of Theravāda Buddhism and the "Little Tradition" of animistic folk-religion. He thought that an wholistic comprehension of the religion of the Burmese people would do empirical justice to the real unity of the upper and lower "parts of an integrated religious system," and <u>historical</u> justice to the development of the system which gradually combined "Buddhism and other religious elements" into a "peculiarly Burmese" religious whole which is not readily identifiable by references to any scripture, and therefore could be labelled, "for want of an established term," as "Burmese religion."

He noted that "the traditional religion" of Burms, that is, "Burmese religion," must have evolved through the historic circumstances, processes and events by which "a more ancient and less organized faith"- namely, "Burmese animism" - had become sycretically integrated with the "more recent, philosophically ordered, and canonical Buddhist faith". This duality, moreover, contrasts the adherents of the Burmese religion who have espoused "the larger share" of the <u>Theravāda Buddhist component</u> in their religion with the majority who have held the "peasant superstitions" belonging to its "Little Tradition" <u>animistic component</u>. But there are problems with this dualization. It may be objected that the religion of Burma's "social elite" and the "peasant superstitions" of the common-folk are not historically distinctive traditions but are aspects of the same complex reality which are conceptually distinguishable in contrastive terms with Theravāda Buddhism, and empirically in terms of Burmese supernaturalism. The Burmese religion does not show that Theravāda Buddhism did not exist at arm's length from the Burmese religion but filled it out by way of scriptural, ritual, ideological, and institutional resources, and by becoming acculturatively merged with and into Burma's aboriginal religion in the course of historically unfolding as the "Burmese" mode of Theravāda Buddhism.

In other words, the Burmese religion presently shows that Theravāda Buddhism could not have become a truly "Burmese" Buddhist tradition unless it was adopted into a "more ancient, less organized faith" of the Burmese people. The fact of this adoption was admitted by Brohm (1963:155, 156, and 167) who observed that the majority of the Burmese "certainly regard themselves as Theravāda Buddhists" and suppose their religion to be "Theravāda Buddhism." In this case, there seems little justification for calling their Theravāda Buddhism by another name - "Burmese religion" - in order to protect the scholarly tradition about the separate existence and different historical development in Burma of its normative and its aboriginal religions. Instead, it would seem more appropriate for the distinctive "Burmese" formulation of the Theravāda Buddhist religion to be recognized, so that its history could be recorded as one regional chapter in the larger historiography of Theravāda Buddhist expansion and growth in South and Southeast Asia. This "history," moreover, would not show the undulating course of a Great Tradition surviving the "vicissitudes" of its passage from mainland India into mainland Southeast Asia, as envisaged by Melford E. Spiro, but the syncretic variegations arising within the Theravāda Buddhism on account of its acculturation with Burma's aboriginal and indigenous religious systems.

C. The "Ordinary" and "Extraordinary" Normative Buddhism of the Burmese

The necessity of an historical perspective in the sociology of Burmese religion is a crucial methodological issue in Melford E. Spiro's major study of Burmese Buddhism (1970). Although Spiro referred to Brohm's work, Michael Ames' systematic characterization of the Sinhalese religion provided the primary model for his psychologistic anthropological study of the Burmese religion. Like Brohm, his primary interest was in the animistic features of the Burmese religion although his viewpoint was closer to Ames' concerning the relation of Animism to Theravāda Buddhism in the religion of Burma. Moreover, Spiro, like Ames, drew highly contrastive dualistic distinctions between the principal systemic components and expression of the religion of Burma's Buddhists.

Spiro's Redfieldian stance toward the religions is indicated by the title which he gave to his second major work on Buddhism and Society: A Great Tradition and its Burmese Vicissitudes (1970). Spiro had projected this as the second of a trio on Burmese Theravāda Buddhism, Burmese Supernaturalism, and Burmese Magical-Animism. His major study of Burmese supernaturalism was published in 1967, and Buddhism and Society in 1970. In the later (1970:3), Spiro explicitly enunciated his theoretical assumptions, his methodological parameters, and his psychologistic anthropological approach. He defined his approach as "an anthropological treatment of Buddhism" primarily in Burma but also in the rest of Theravāda Buddhist South Asia and as having its starting point "where the textual and the historical scholar ends." This suggests that Spiro may have thought of his anthropological study of Burmese religion as being a transcending scientific advancement upon the historical study of Theravāda Buddhism.

But in Buddhism and Society (1970:4-5) he expanded the definition of his methodology to cover both the anthropological and the historical approaches to Burmese Buddhism. His ground for doing so was in order to correct shortcomings in recent anthropological studies

in regard to the historical bearings of the contemporary
Buddhist South Asian religions being studied. "With
some few exceptions," he observed, "modern
anthropologists who study the beliefs and rituals of
practicing Buddhists, have . . . ignored the normative
sources from which they derive." They have accordingly
represented the contemporary forms of Buddhist South
Asia's "traditional" religions in opposition to the
normative forms of those religions which interest
academic historians, thereby creating interpretational
problems in regard to the character and development of
the religions which have "seldom been confronted."[4]

Spiro perceived these problems within the
anthropological science as being resolvable so long as
the socio-scientific exploration of Buddhist South Asian
religions encompasses: (i) the socio-cultural
interpretation and explanation of the ancient Theravāda
Buddhist "textual doctrines" which contemporary popular
Buddhist beliefs and practices express; (ii)
consideration of Buddhist canonical doctrines and other
features of the ancient Theravāda Buddhist tradition
which have apparently become forgotten, ignored,
obsolescent, or rejected by Buddhists in contemporary
Buddhist South Asia; and (iii) examination of "non-
Buddhist" and "non-normative" Buddhist beliefs and
practices which the Burmese have assimilated with their
Theravāda Buddhist beliefs and practices.

Spiro accordingly envisaged the anthropological
study of "traditional" religion in Burma and elsewhere
as having an essential "historical perspective" which
would complement and even advance the purely "academical
historical study" of the religions applied to Theravāda
Buddhism by members of the older school of Buddhist
textual-historical studies. Spiro (1970:4) contended

that any purely "structural-functional" approach to the sociology of Buddhist belief and practice in Southeast Asia lacking specific references to their historic roots in the normative tradition of Theravāda Buddhism would be empirically unsound. For Theravāda Buddhism has been the source from which the popular beliefs and practices of the religion have derived their "motivational and cognitive bases." Spiro (1970:15) also insisted that: "If religion is to be studied as a living system rather than exclusively as a body of canonical doctrines, [then] it must be studied in [both] its historical and cultural contexts."

Spiro (1970:11) thought that this would require "normative Buddhism" to be recognized historically as "a child of ancient Indian culture" which emerged outside of India as "the ordinary norm . . . intended for the religious majority" and as "the extraordinary norm . . . confined to a much smaller group . . . whose primary concern was with salvation."But he also recognized this doubly-normative Theravāda Buddhism as one among several "traditional religions" of ancient India which had acquired "ordinary" and "extraordinary" normative expressions in the beliefs and practices of South and Southeast Asia's Theravāda Buddhists. However, just as Theravāda Buddhism survived outside of India as the "extraordinary normative Buddhism" of Buddhist South Asia's elites of monks and scholars and intellectuals and still "persists today as the religion of those Buddhists who aspire to [the] soteriological goal," one must assume also that it has flourished as the "ordinary normative Buddhism" of the majority of Buddhist South Asian peoples who perceive themselves as "Theravāda Buddhists" and their religion as Theravāda Buddhism.

Spiro's distinctions between "ordinary" and "extraordinary" normative Theravāda Buddhism in mainland Southeast Asia are problematic for an academic history of the religion. The historians have regularly represented "Theravāda Buddhism" in terms of its "extraordinary normative expression." But the distinction is also as an interpretational problem for sociologists in the light of the extraordinary and ordinary normative forms and expressions of the Theravāda Buddhism in South Asia showing their melding with aboriginal pre-Buddhist religions of South and Southeast Asia. This indicates that the resolution of the problems of both schools required a broader definition of Theravāda Buddhism which incorporates all the expressional transformations comprising the historical career of Buddhism in South and Southeast Asia.

However, despite these crucially important historical considerations, Spiro was primarily interested in anthropological questions and concerns relating to the everyday Buddhism of Burma's Theravāda Buddhists. Without identifying this everyday Buddhism as "Theravāda Buddhism," he undertook a systemic characterization of its structure and a psychologistic explanation of the functional interrelations of its component subsystems. He perceived the religion of the Burmese as being basically a "village-religion system" espoused by a Burmese population which is "85 percent rural" yet also embraces a "body of canonical doctrines." The system, moreover, "happens to be the typical general expression of the religion" which is actively present also in the "typically Buddhist urban centres" of Burma, such as Mandalay, as well as in typical Burmese villages such as Yeigyi. Furthermore, since the <u>urban</u> Buddhism in Burma differs little from the Buddhism of Burma's villages, it also is "typical" for the whole of Buddhist Burma. This religion of Burma's Theravāda Buddhists as a whole is an historic actuality which can be interpreted through sociological and historical generalizations about the Theravāda Buddhism of the whole of Buddhist South Asia in regard to its complex character and to the factors in its regional development following its expansion from mainland India into mainland Southeast Asia.

Throughout the nineteen-sixties and seventies, South Asia's historic Theravāda Buddhism presented a complexity demanding socio-historical explanation. The failure of any satisfactory explanational outcome during the period was due to a fault in the socio-scientific study of traditional Theravāda Buddhism itself and principally due to defective uses of the Redfield-Marriott dichotomy in the socio-historical interpretation of the religion. Nevertheless, a movement toward an historical explanation arose through the maturation of the sociological study of Theravāda Buddhism making increasing room for historical considerations in sociological data and for their coalescence into an adumbrated "socio-history" of Theravāda Buddhism. Spiro's work was in the vanguard of this historical perspective. It outstandingly reflects a stage or phase in the scientific movement from a-historical structural-functionalism toward the "socio-history" of Buddhism in South and Southeast Asia. His psychologistically-oriented structural-functionalist study of the Burmese religion significantly advanced Ames' sociological "survey" of the Sinhalese religious system. Its springboard was a statement by John F. Embree (1945:213) that we can never learn the nature of

a religion simply by perusing its sacred texts or
written words "torn from their social context." Textual
studies have to be complemented by "historical and
exegetical studies of Buddhist scripture, philosophical
analyses of Buddhist doctrines, or descriptions of the
historical career of Buddhism." These are important for
social scientists because they are introductory to those
special concerns which anthropologists have when they
explore the relations between scriptural texts "and the
more general ordering of social and cultural life" in
Buddhist Asia.

Despite these historiographical considerations,
however, (1970:4) Spiro maintained the primary
anthropological interest in the folk-religion of Burma's
Theravāda Buddhists for which he distinguished the
Theravāda Buddhist theology and philosophy from "the
generality of Theravāda Buddhist ideas and beliefs"
comprising the regional and local forms in "the
religious system of Theravāda Buddhists" observed in
Cambodia, Laos, Ceylon, Burma, and Thailand. He
referred to this religion as their "Theravāda Buddhist
religion" and as the "real, historic, Theravāda
Buddhism" of Buddhist South Asia's peasant-majority of
"Theravāda Buddhists." Furthermore, he contrasted this
popular Theravāda Buddhism with the "normative Theravāda
Buddhism" presented by the Pali Buddhist canonical
literature and the professional Theravāda Buddhist
Saṅgha while recognizing also their integral
relationship in terms of the "real" the "ideal," the
"actual" and the "doctrinal," and the "existential"
versus the "normative" expressions of the belief-system.

Spiro perceived these contrastive relations as a
"set of discrepancies" in the complexity of the
religion. He perceived that they could not be

scientifically <u>explained</u> within the complexity of the belief-system without a complementary explanation of how Buddhists have simultaneously espoused ideologically contradictory and functionally different religious value-systems without forming compartmentalized and partisan sectarian factions. Yet the "discrepancies" and "contradictions" also indicate an historical problem in regard to any socio-cultural conditions, processes, and events in the religion's historic past which could have generated these multivalent features in the religious tradition of Burma's Theravāda Buddhism, or, in Spiro's words, could have transformed "a novel and great revolutionary religion like Buddhism" into the religious "status quo" in contemporary Buddhist Burma.

Spiro (1970:5) looked for a socio-historical answer to the anthropological and the historical problems primarily in "the social actors" whose religious mentality reflects the subconscious integration of the "Great Tradition" of Theravāda Buddhism with their ancient, pre-Buddhist, religious "Little Tradition." In this connection, he had delimited the definition of the religious "Great Tradition" of the Burmese people to the normative or canonical Theravāda Buddhist ideological system. He admitted that this particularization is problematic, not least because "a number of religion-scholars gravely doubt that the normative Theravāda Buddhism . . . can legitimately be designated a religion at all" and can be religiously contrasted with the manifold of "non-normative beliefs and practices" of the Burmese which "diverge from the canonical doctrine." He supposed that the relationship between Theravāda Buddhism and the religion of Burma's Theravāda Buddhists could be usefully compared with Catholicism and Protestantism in contemporary Christianity contrasting the classical with the popular modes and expressions of the religion, and specifically the historic scripturalistic and monastic tradition of "normative Theravāda Buddhism" and the lay forms of the tradition, in both their earlier and their "more recent historical expressions". But his reductionistic representation of the classical tradition also displayed interpretational incongruities showing Theravāda Buddhism as a "scriptural tradition" which is both atheistic and religious, and being supported and adopted by, yet ideologically different from and even opposed to, the religion of "the numbers of Theravāda Buddhists" and members of other [Buddhist] societies in Buddhist South Asia who happen to be also "devotees of other religions" to which they "resort for supernatural assistance in their quest for salvation." In other words, Spiro's representation of the religion of Burma's Theravāda Buddhists could not integrally cover all of its expressions, particularly any version of it espoused by the majority of Burma's Theravāda Buddhists who, as Spiro observed, rarely "internalize the canonical doctrines, which therefore, are either ignored or rejected by the faithful."

D. The Supernaturalistic Dimension of Burmese Theravāda Buddhism

One confusing feature of Spiro's anthropological exposition of the religion of Burma's Theravāda Buddhists was his observation that the canonical Buddhism is not their only "normative Buddhism." "The faithful . . . have [also] acquired other additional forms of Buddhism which for them are equally, or nearly equally, normative." He distinguished three principal forms of this "normative Buddhism": nibbanic-Buddhism which is soteriologically concerned with release from

the cycle of Rebirth; <u>kammatic</u>-Buddhism, which is
concerned with release from the baneful conditions of
human everyday life; and "apotropaic" Buddhism which is
a non-soteriological religion concerned with "man's
worldly welfare" particularly through protections from
physical hurts and dangers. He perceived these as
<u>conceptually-distinguishable</u> forms which do not indicate
<u>historically distinct</u> traditions or presuppose that
Burma's Buddhists practice three kinds of Buddhism.
They are, instead, analytical distinctions drawn out of
the "bewildering hodgepodge" of "canonical" and "non-
canonical" beliefs and practices in the real religion of
Burma's Buddhist peoples who have adopted "in varying
degrees" systems of doctrines and attitudes reflecting
all three types of "normative Buddhism."[5]

Yet even the conceptual distinctions carry
historical implications specifically in regard to the
conditions and causes behind the multi-dimensional
character and pluriform complexity of Burmese Theravāda
Buddhism. This complexity, moreover, casts doubt upon
the historical validity of any account of Theravāda
Buddhism in Burma based solely on the supposition that
it is an atheistic philosophical system enshrined in a
corpus of canonical scriptures and expressed by the
meditational practices of a minority monastic-elite.
The authentic history would have to represent the
integral totality of all the component systems and
subsystems of the religion and their historic
expressions in space and in time including those
expressions which show the syncretic amalgamations of
imported Buddhist systems with indigenous, aboriginal,
pre-Buddhist and non-Buddhist religion in Burma.

The demand for an wholistic history of Burmese
Theravāda Buddhism makes the historicalization of

Spiro's conceptualistic compartmentalization of the Burmese religion into a "pure Buddhism" separated from the aboriginal religious superstitions of the Burmese masses untenable. The complexity of Theravāda Buddhism in Burma rules out Spiro's notion that Theravāda Buddhism maintained its separate identity and historically survived "the vicissitudes" of its popular adoption by the Burmese. His introduction to Buddhism and Society indicates that his unhistorical compartmentalization was rooted in his methodological scheme for a "projected three-volume study of Burma" beginning with Burmese Supernaturalism (1967), followed by Buddhism and Society (1970) focussed mainly on Theravāda Buddhism in Burma, and a final volume on Burmese Magical-Animism. Spiro (1967:2) evidently assumed the empirical actuality of his compartmentalizations on the grounds of the "truism" that the peoples of Asia are heirs to more than one religious tradition and practice different and logically incompatible religious systems. His knowledge of McKim Marriott's theory of the syncretistic dynamic of "Sanskritization/Buddhaization" and "parochialization" in ancient India should have given him a different viewpoint on the one religion formed by syncretistic absorptions and submergences of systems that were previously historically distinctive and unfolded the polylithic metasystems of religious belief and practice comprising "Sanskritic Hinduism" in India and the "Theravāda Buddhist religion" in the "Theravāda Buddhist countries" of South and Southeast Asia.

Spiro assumed, in Burmese Supernaturalism (1967), that the "folk religion" or "supernaturalism" practiced by the Burmese is distinct from their Theravāda Buddhism and yet is synergistically related to it. This assumption, in turn, ruled out the probability that this "supernaturalism" could have been part of the folk Theravāda Buddhism. Instead, Spiro attributed a religious pluralism to Burma's Theravāda Buddhist population in terms of a simultaneous following of three distinctive religions: Buddhism, Supernaturalism, and Animism. This distinction provided no room for conceding that their religion comprises an wholistic syncretic amalgam of different religious strains indicated by the supernaturalistic features evidently present in the Theravāda Buddhism of the Burmese, and by their Theravāda Buddhist cosmology which had long become expanded into the full-blown Burmese pantheon of Buddhist and buddhaized traditional-Burmese deities. Spiro (1967:5) insisted instead that "Buddhism" and "Supernaturalism" in Burma connote "very different religions" presenting oppositional interpretations of human suffering and incompatible "techniques for its resolution."

A contrary viewpoint, however, appears in Spiro's admission that his conceptual differentiations between "Buddhism" and "Supernaturalism" are not empirically based since there are not two traditions which the Burmese recognize and simultaneously espouse and no imaginational distinction between "Buddhist" and "non-Buddhist" forms of their religion. Nor do they differentiate between the supposed "this-worldly" concerns of their supernaturalism and the suppositional "other-worldly" concerns of their Buddhism indicated by Michael Ames. While there are contrastive concerns and interests, these are complementarily integrated within a unified religious consciousness and its expressions showing the interchangeabilities of the idealistic and the pragmatical, or sacred and profane concerns, or the

soteriological and the materialistic motivations behind
their rituals. Their "Burmese religion" accordingly
embraces the furthest esoteric, supernaturalistic and
animistic reaches of their ritualistic recourse.
Moreover, the religion's supernaturalistic and animistic
features which primarily serve their "this-worldly"
needs and concerns, and the philosophical and doctrinal
references which address their "other-worldly" hopes and
aspirations, never do so exclusively. The doctrine and
the ritual, and the philosophy and the supernaturalism,
have interchangeable significations within the this-
worldly and other-worldly functions and objectives of
their Theravāda Buddhism. The conceptual distinctions
which the historian and the sociologist have made
between "Theravāda Buddhism" and "Magical-animism," do
not have historical counterparts in the real religion of
the Burmese except as facets of a polydimensional
historic tradition.

Although Spiro's study of Burmese Supernaturalism
can be faulted on account of his historical
empiricalization of conceptually differentiated
religious systems, it has significant bearings upon the
supernaturalistic character of the Theravāda Buddhism of
the Burmese. In it, a theoretical exposition of the
religious genre of "supernaturalism" is used for
introducing an empirical characterization of its
historic Burmese expressions. In it, Spiro stated its
primary purpose as being the purely "scientific"
interest of testing and validating a particular socio-
anthropological theory in the light of a presently
existent "type" of religious organization within the
"class" of "supernaturalism." He nevertheless
recognized the scientific uniqueness of the Burmese
"type" due to its distinctive "Burmese" socio-cultural

and traditional contexts as well as its general character as a contemporary reflection of "universal processes and functions" characterizing the general "supernaturalistic subclass" of religions. He also supposed that the "contextual Burmese range of explanations" of this sub-class would "validate" the current anthropological conception and theory of "supernaturalism" through empirical comparisons and contrastings of its distinctive "Burmese" and "Buddhist" manifestations, while the "traditional" features of the Burmese "supernaturalism" would illuminate the scientific "historical understanding" of the religious totality in contemporary Burma.

Spiro (1967:3) defined Burmese supernaturalism as "a variety of 'supernatural' beliefs [about] ghosts, demons, witches, and those spirits whom the Burmese call nats." He indicated the character of these nats as "evil spirits" having "the form of humans" and possessing supernatural power to cause suffering. He called the system of ritual-appeasement of the nats as "the nat cultus"; and he indicated a typical locus for the belief and the practices as a village of upper Burma located approximately ten miles from the city of Mandalay and pseudonymously called Yeigyi.[6] He thought that the "structure" of its "supernaturalism" could be represented in Straussian socio-cultural terms as a psycho-social "map" showing its ideological and cosmological superstructure, its animistic substructure, its diverse systemic patterns, and any other features of the totality in the religious understanding and behaviour of the Burmese people within and beyond Yeigyi.

Spiro expected such a psycho-social mapping of the Burmese supernaturalism to display clearly the

buddhaization of its pantheonic superstructure in which
are related to the divine Buddha an hierarchical
descending-order of Buddhas, deities, bodhisattva-s,
arhat-s, monks, and laity, followed by the lower orders
of sub-human animal, plant, and other natural beings and
on down to the lowest orders of demonic and animistic
subterrestrial beings. But Spiro's schematic
representation of the system seems more rigidly
compartmentalized than is so in the cosmological scheme
of the Burmese. For while the Buddhist degree of
buddhaization of a higher or lesser being is governed by
its proximity to the supreme Buddha in the mythic system
of the Burmese religion, this is never static since
beings appear to ascend and descend the ladder of
buddhahood in the cosmological mythic tradition.

Furthermore, the nats, whom Spiro conceptually
placed outside of Burmese Buddhism are an intrinsic
feature of the same cosmological system and have their
own hierarchy of greater or lesser buddhahood or mythic
proximity to the Buddha and his agents. In this scheme,
accordingly, the nat cultus does not comprise the ritual
component of a religious system which is historically
distinct from Burmese Buddhism, but is the animistic
component of a Buddhist metasystem which has also
"supernaturalistic" and other generic components.
Spiro's rigid categorizations of "nat-propitiators,"
"supernaturalists," and "Buddhists" among Burma's
Buddhist population appears in this light to lack
empirical justification even despite any justifying
claims based on his "research procedure" comprising
"information-gathering" by means of a house-to-house
"census." The record of the procedure indicates a
somewhat sparse amount of esoteric information on
spiritism among the peasant-folk of Yeigyi supplemented

by Spiro's participant observation in several unusual
"supernatural rituals" of exorcism and divination, and
in "three important nat festivals" interpreted by
"shamans." His information does not indicate a complete
and distinctive religious system. At best it indicates
a shamanistic element in the supernaturalism of Burma's
rural Buddhists, not the comprehensive nat-religion
which Spiro found replete with a distinctive belief-
system, ritual organization, calendar of diurnal, lunar,
seasonal, annual, regional, and domestic festivals, and
functioning in tandem with the complementative higher
religious systems of nibbanic, kammatic, and
"apotropaic" Buddhism.[7]

On the whole, it is the intrinsic unity of the
religion of Burma's Buddhist population which is the
real obstacle in Spiro's compartmentalistic approach to
its interpretation and explanation. Spiro (1967: 264-
271) shows he was aware of this unity inasmuch as the
majority of Burmese espouse only one religion which they
have traditionally identified as Theravāda Buddhism. He
also followed the procedure of other sociologists of the
region in explaining the inner complexity of this
unified system in structuralistic terms of the
ideological and functional networks interconnecting
diverse and even contradictory components. But he did
not avoid the pitfall of confusing the conceptual
differentiations with historical ones and thereby
creating the image of a complex of ideologically
contradictory and functionally complementary religions
instead of recognizing a real core-tradition whose
divergent historic expressions can be arranged along a
continuum of contemporaneous variations connecting its
animistic and supernaturalistic formulations at one end

of the polar extreme and its ideologically abstracted "canonical" formulation at the other.

This arrangement, which was first indicated by Michael Ames in regard to the Sinhalese Buddhist complex, would have required Spiro's recognition of the dynamic relationship of "continuity" and "transformation" in the temporal and spacial development of Theravāda Buddhism which S.J. Tambiah expounded so profoundly in regard to religion in Thailand. It would have integrated his perception of the urbane and peasant dimensions and expressions of Theravāda Buddhism and have prevented Spiro's conception of an intellectualistically remote Theravāda Buddhism which managed to survive the "vicissitudes" of its adoptions by the general population of Burma. He had paved the way for an integral historical viewpoint by indicating in psychologistic terms "the lexical incorporation" of the "Buddhist devas" into "the indigenous religious terminology" of the Burmese people, and of "the aboriginal nats" into the "indigenous cognitive structure" of their Burmese formulation of Buddhism. In this connection, Spiro appears to have presented a specific formulation of McKim Marriott's general theory of the acculturational mechanisms of "buddhaization" and "parochialization" by which a Buddhist deva-system could have become assimilated with an aboriginal Burmese "nat cultus."[8]

On the other hand, his distancing of "Theravāda Buddhism" from the mainstream of this buddhaizational-parochializational process prevented his admission of the most important of the implicit conclusions of Marriott's integrational dynamics, namely, how Theravāda Buddhism became a syncretized religious complex by being brought into and merged with and accommodated to the pre-Buddhist aboriginal religions of the Burmese population. Instead, this hypothetical syncretization of Theravāda Buddhism was apparently ruled out of Spiro's presentation on the relationship of "supernaturalism" with Buddhism in Burma which was based, not on historical scholarship about contemporary Buddhism in Burma, but on the professed "opinion" of "the vast majority of Burmese Buddhists," including "even peasants . . . [and] intellectuals as well," that the two are structurally distinct religions "in a state of [mutual] tension."

The scientific hypothesis versus the brute fact tested Spiro's interpretive acumen. Spiro (1967:251-252) acknowledged that, "contrary to some Buddhist intellectuals and to most western critics of Burmese nats, animistic beliefs, as well as ritual, are perfectly compatible with orthodox Buddhism, even with Buddhism of the Pali canon." Even so, "this is not to say . . . that there are no grounds on which Buddhism and animism are incompatible"; on the contrary, "there are grounds for conflict between these two systems, and there is abundant evidence that the Burmese themselves, at least the more introspective ones, are aware of such a conflict."[9] On the other hand, they are apparently interrelated though not "hopelessly intertwined"; they are not components "forming a syncretistic religion"- citing Brohm (1963:165) - yet nor are they "two separate religions" even though they are analytically distinguishable. There is no underlying non-Buddhist religion surmounted by a "veneer of Buddhism" - citing Temple and Scott - but instead, a pragmatical partnership of Buddhist religion with animistic non-religion which is supported by an ascertainable "division of labor" wherein the "Great Tradition"

Buddhism has the principal and primary status and role and the "Little Tradition" of Burmese supernaturalism a subordinate adjunctive functionality.[10]

Such dichotomies, in the end, are unsatisfactory because they fly in the face of the integral, organic unity of the historic religion of Burma's Buddhist population. Recognition of them seems to be a concession to contemporary social scientists and their scientific theories, not deductions from evidence behind empirically-informed field-researches on Burmese Buddhism. Nevertheless, Spiro made a substantial contribution toward an wholistic socio-historical explanation of the Buddhist religious complex in South Asia, while its faults were to inspire the magnificent microscopic and macroscopic analysis and survey of the Thai Buddhist totality which became the central objective of Tambiah's work throughout the nineteen-seventies.

Chapter Four. The Transformational Process in Thai Theravāda Buddhism

Applications of the Redfield-Marriott "Great Tradition" and "Little Tradition" dichotomy to the religions of Buddhist South Asia reached a peak of analytical and interpretational sophistication toward the end of the nineteen-seventies. Studies by Stanley J. Tambiah, Charles F. Keyes, and A. Thomas Kirsch particularly indicate a movement beyond Redfield's paradigm of peasant socio-cultures toward a socio-historical paradigm and a shift of emphasis from structural functionalism to socio-cultural historicism. In this regard, Thailand's religious complex provided a testing-ground for the Great Tradition/Little Tradition dichotomy's applications to its historic and contemporary social expressions particularly in respect of the "State Buddhism" and the "Little Tradition" folk-religion of Thailand's Theravāda Buddhists.

Tambiah and his contemporaries distinguished three Buddhisms within the complexity of the Thai religion. The most striking is the royal Buddhism of the Thai Buddhist nation-state as it had developed through the fusion of the Mahāyāna and the Theravāda Buddhist systems shortly after the political unification of the Thai, Cambodian, and Laotian peoples in the former Cambodian state. Next, they recognized the "popular Buddhism" of Thailand appearing as an extension among Thailand's rural peasant-folk of an urban monastic Buddhism disconnected from the Buddhist-state cult. Thirdly, they recognized a contemporaneous "folk-Buddhism" having an aboriginal animistic substructure and a supernaturalistic superstructure suffused with elements of Thailand's popular, state, and canonical Buddhisms.

This Thai religious complex, of course, indicated a

regional form of Theravāda Buddhism in South Asia differing fundamentally from the normative and canonical tradition espoused by the Buddhist elites. It seemed inexplicable, sociologically and historically, solely in Buddhist terms, neither completely in contrast to the normative Theravāda Buddhism, nor entirely in non-Buddhist terms of brahmanic and aboriginal religious traditions which became suffused by later accretions of Theravāda Buddhist features and elements. Hence its complexity presented special methodological problems which Tambiah and others addressed in prefaces to their scientific explorations of Buddhism in Thailand.

A. Methodological Criteria for a Socio-History of Buddhism exemplified by Thailand

S.J. Tambiah's important studies of Thai religion stem from the socio-cultural anthropologies of Paul Mus and Robert Redfield. Although Tambiah published his major study of Thai supernaturalism during his appointment as Lecturer in Anthropology at the University of Cambridge between 1964 and 1971, the complementary inputs of Paul Mus' anthropo-historicism and Robert Redfield's socio-historical concepts of "Great Tradition" and "Little Tradition" applied to peasant socio-cultures in Hindu and Buddhist South Asia are prominent throughout his socio-scientific study of Thai religion. But it is in his earlier major work during the nineteen-sixties and seventies and published as Buddhism and the Spirit Cults in North-east Thailand (1970) that the influence of Redfield's methodological theory and techniques for the socio-historical study of religions is most apparent. Redfield's influence is less evident in his later work and almost disappears in his crowning study titled World Conqueror and World Renouncer (1976) and sub-titled "A Study of Buddhism and Polity in Thailand against a Historical Background."

His earlier and later work, accordingly, display the
general "shift" in Redfieldian concepts and theory in
the sociological study of religions of South and
Southeast Asia which developed during the nineteen-
sixties and seventies. The "shift" occurred as a
gradual advancement of "historical" over "structural"
considerations in socio-anthropological interpretations
of traditional religions in Buddhist South Asia. In
this respect, Tambiah's work is notable on account of
his wholistic perspective on "the total field" of the
Thai religion and methodological application to it of
synchronic and diachronic concepts. His advancement of
the scientific study of contemporary expressions of
"traditional" religious meta-systems can be demonstrated
by a detailed exposition of his two most important works
showing positions he adopted and maintained even in his
most recent writings.

In Buddhism and the Spirit Cults, he selected the
ritual-complex in Thai-village religion as the arena in
which the Redfieldian conceptual categories and
methodological criteria could be demonstrably applied in
the socio-anthropological study of folk-religion.
Tambiah showed that the Thai ritual-network comprises
four distinct religious subsystems whose relationships
are interpretable through synchronic categories of
opposition, complementarity, linkage, and hierarchy, and
whose interrelational developments are explicable
through the diachronic categories of continuity and
transformation. He applied these concepts
interpretively to the ritual system for the purpose of
explaining the total "traditional-religion system" in
Thailand as it presently is. But he also thought that
the socio-anthropological understanding of such
complexes could be advanced if the current historical
science on Buddhism were consulted with a view to

showing how this rural and peasant-folk reality is related to Thailand's long religious past.

In World Conqueror and World Renouncer (1976), however, Tambiah set out to show how the relationship of the Thai Buddhist Sangha to the Thai society, to the Thai Buddhist kingship, and to the Thai Buddhist national polity could be synchronically interpreted in terms of coexistent cosmological, spacial, temporal and politico-economic "levels of meaning," and be diachronically interpreted in terms of the continuities and transformations which unfolded contemporary Thailand's national Buddhism.

A keynote of Tambiah's socio-scientific interpretation of Thai Buddhism and its relations was his keen appreciation of the historical factors which shaped its present complexity, that is, the essential bearings of an historical perspective for any empirically-sound sociological interpretation and explanation of a religion whose present complexity is a culmination of its preceding transformations. His development of "the socio-historical approach" to the contemporary forms of historic religious systems also brought to a head certain methodological tendencies which are found in Heinz Bechert's monumental study of Buddhism and State polity in the Theravāda countries of South and Southeast Asia (1966, 1967, and 1973). Tambiah built on Bechert's understanding of the Thai religious complexity. B.J. Terwiel's theoretical preface for A. Thomas Kirsch's essay on "Complexity in the Thai Religious System: An Interpretation" (1977) extended Tambiah's study of the ritual to the total Thai religious system but for the purpose of resolving the "discrepancy" in recent sociological "analyses of contemporary Theravada Buddhism" concerning how the Buddhist/non-Buddhist, Animistic/Supernaturalistic, and other "strands of religion" or "different subsystems" are interrelated. However, whereas Terwiel psychologistically interpreted these component "strands" as projections of mental "compartmentalizations," Kirsch interpreted them sociologically as "variables" wrought by socio-cultural forces in the changing "historical circumstances" of South and Southeast Asia's Theravāda Buddhist countries.

An important acknowledgement of Tambiah's pioneering methodological contributions to the socio-scientific study of religions appeared in the review by Frank Reynolds (1978) of Tambiah's World Conqueror and World Renouncer. Reynolds appreciated the wholistic perspective in Tambiah's projected overview and analysis of contemporary Thailand's historic religion, and his balancing a microscopic analysis of Thai rural religion by a macroscopic "survey" of the total Buddhist "field" in rural and urban Thailand. Reynolds appreciated the scientific exactitude of Tambiah's "three basic methodological emphases" upon "on the scene observations," historical explanations, and structural-historical explanation using basic synchronic and diachronic categories. He acknowledged the "particular integrity" of Tambiah's "quite self-conscious" interpretational predilections in regard to the ritual, the mythic, and "the mytho-historic strands" of Thailand's Theravāda Buddhist heritage, and his "focusing on characteristic complementarities and tensions within and among various levels of religious, political, and social meaning and activity" which display "the richness, diversity, and flexibility of the Theravāda and the Thai traditions." He commended Tambiah's distinctive syncretic "structural/historical approach" not only to the living Thai religious tradition but also to the normative Buddhist tradition as it "has been appropriated by those who wrote the classical historical chronicles." He particularly lauded Tambiah's selective "inclusion of a variety of interesting and provocative cross-cultural comparisons" of the Theravada "Sangha and polity paradigm" respective to Śrī Laṅka, Burma, and Thailand, and his unique expositions of the "exclusive categories" and "irreconcilable dichotomies" found in the doctrinal and institutional systems of Buddhism, Hinduism, Christianity, and Islam.

Martin Barber and Victor King (1973), and Reynolds also, found fault with Tambiah's exposition of Thai supernaturalism. Reynold's critique is particularly cogent because he was familiar also with the work of Tambiah's mentor in socio-cultural anthropology, Paul Mus, and this background-knowledge specially equipped him for evaluating Tambiah's distinctive combination of the anthropology of Paul Mus and of Robert Redfield in his socio-historical study of Thai religion.[1] In a later independent study of Mus' work, Reynolds (1981:228f.) explained that Mus rejected "the commonly held belief that the religious history of India and the religious history of Indianized Southeast Asia are radically different." On the contrary, they "involve the same basic components and processes." Moreover, the two histories are amenable to the same "holistic mode of interpretation" which requires "the identification of [the] central patterns of thought, action, and experience" expressed in their philosophy, ritual and art, an exposition of "the various 'logics' that inform those patterns and make them operational," and the "elucidation of the relevant historical processes and developments" through which "the basic patterns and logics" behind the respective religious traditions have become historically "elaborated."[2]

Reynolds noticed that Mus had been specially interested in the developmental processes occurring through interchanges of "new and foreign elements" with existing patterns of a religious system, and in showing how the "basic pattern or logic" is "preserved and enriched" even while a tradition may be unfolding also "a radically new version" of its system.[3] Mus had found historically significant illustrations of these transformations in the early development of Buddhism in ancient India, and in the "major process" which led to the historic culminations of the Hīnayāna and the Mahāyāna patterns of the Buddhist appropriation of specifically selected brahmanical symbols and cults of royalty. Reynolds thought that Mus perceived this buddhaization of brahmanical elements as an indication that "the common Buddhism" which developed alongside, or later than, the monastic Buddhism could not have "come into its own" as "a fully blown reformulation and extension of the patterns and logic . . . central to the indigenous and Brahmanic traditions" of ancient India and Indianized Southeast Asia, but as a melding of their respective "basic patterns" and "logic" into locally formulated "new versions" of Buddhism. Accordingly, "the Mahāyāna and Hīnayāna traditions" could not have preserved their basic patterns and logics unchanged throughout the course of their temporal and spacial expansions in South and Southeast Asia. Nor could they have survived and developed without the transformations consequent upon their incorporation of new and foreign religious elements along the corridors of their expansion throughout and beyond mainland India.[4]

Tambiah (1976:3) thoroughly understood these ideas. He particularly utilized Mus' theory of the "religious and symbolic dynamic" effecting the historical process of basic pattern change and development in religions. He adopted Mus' socio-historical account of political Buddhism in Aśoka's India and its later forms in Buddhist South Asia where Mahāyāna and Hīnayāna traditions merged into a state-buddhism through their "appropriation of [brahmanic] royal elements from the third century B.C. Moreover, Mus' explanation of the dynamic of symbolic and cultic interchange which "eventually led to the Mahāyāna transformation of the [Buddhist] tradition and to the shaping of the normative form of the Hīnayāna tradition, indicated to Tambiah the possible outcomes of the acculturation of these traditions beyond mainland India including "the manner of their taking root" and developing the regional characteristics of their distinctive Sinhalese, Burmese, and Thai versions.[5]

Yet it is apparent also that Tambiah relied upon Robert Redfield's theoretical anthropology for his own distinctive applications of synchronic and diachronic concepts for explaining the mechanisms and outcome of Buddhist acculturation in Thailand. But whereas his earlier major study of Thai supernaturalism displays his confidence in the interpretational applicability of the Redfield-Marriott dichotomy to religions in Buddhist South Asia, his later major work shows doubt amounting to a critique of Redfield's paradigm of peasant socio-cultures and questioning of its viability for an historical explanation of South Asian Buddhism based on the theory of dynamic acculturation of foreign and newly imported religious systems which Redfield's principal associate, McKim Marriott, had developed. Tambiah's later work, accordingly, was both a culmination of the Redfieldian interpretation of Buddhist South Asian religions and its transcendence by a new yet only tentative socio-historical paradigm.

Tambiah's evaluation of the Redfield-Marriott dichotomy began as a critique and attempted improvement of the paradigm in view of misleading generalizations which it generated in regard to the character and development of religions in Buddhist South Asia. It proceeded toward a replacement of the analytical uses of the paradigm by interpretive uses toward an organically wholistic representation of Buddhist South Asia's religious metasystems. It culminated in the tentative replacement of its structuralistic perspective by a socio-historical or cultural-historical perspective or system of concepts and theory on the contemporary forms of traditional religions and their developmental historical backdrops.

The starting-point of Tambiah's replacement of the Redfield-Marriott dichotomy was a discussion of its applications to Sanskritic-Hinduism by Dumont and Pocock. Their critique formed a substantial part of Chapter Twenty-one of Tambiah's work on Buddhism and the Spirit Cults in Northeast Thailand in which Tambiah addressed the problem of how to relate empirical data garnered in the field of contemporary South Asian religious systems "to the religious tradition represented in the literary texts." Tambiah noted that Dumont and Pocock had rejected the answer indicated by Redfield and his associates in terms of a dichotomy of a "great tradition of civilization" interlinked with a "little tradition" of village socio-cultures on the grounds that the "postulated processes" of "universalization" and "parochialization" which Marriott had emphasized are not integral to the civilization but are accidental to "the village and wider civilization." In other words, these diachronic categories do not explain the complexity of the village socio-culture itself. Dumont and Pocock rejected Marriott's proposition of externally-related "Great Tradition" and "Little Tradition" elements in village socio-cultures (although it is not evident that they fully understood Marriott's theory of Great Tradition/Little Tradition interaction). They offered instead a counter-theory of integrated "levels" of ideological organization ranging from the "higher level" of Sanskritic or literary Hinduism to the "lower level" of "popular Hinduism." By insisting, nevertheless, that the two "levels" are somehow "homogeneous," they discounted Marriott's notion of historically autochthonic "traditions." On the other hand, they were also ready to exclude the "Great Tradition" component of the hybrid village socio-culture from their inquiries on the ground that the Sanskritic Hinduism properly interests antiquarians and historians of religions rather than sociologists.

Tambiah, however, did not accept their conclusions without qualifications. He doubted that Dumont and Pocock had fully recognized the organic complexity of the contemporary Hindu village socio-culture whose expressions of a "little tradition," ascertained from empirical data, appear to be integratively related with a "great tradition" represented in literary texts. This integrality denies anthropologists the convenience of excluding the "Great Tradition" component from their inquiries. Tambiah was also dissatisfied with the conceptual distinctions made by anthropologists between the "upper" and the "lower levels" of Hinduism. He thought that the notion of a "higher level" of Hinduism is a socio-scientific "myth" contrived for its hodgepodge of "highly miscellaneous, varied, and non-contemporaneous elements" in a manner which is "in some respects static and profoundly a-historical." He viewed the mythic notion of an all-India "popular Hinduism" also as a contrivance out of "the lowest common denominator of shared Hindu religious beliefs and customs."

Tambiah's understanding of the integral relation of the "canonical" and the "popular" Buddhism in South Asia was the pivot of his criticisms. Tambiah (1970:371) indicated this central issue of his critique as being an historical concern about how "traditional" Hinduism and Buddhism actually developed in South Asia. The empirical soundness and historical validity of "the idea of two levels" appeared to be in question for being "an invention of the anthropologists dictated, not so much by the reality he studies as by his professional perspective." Only one "level" can properly concern anthropologists. This is "the level of reality" comprising "social facts" as one dimension of the socio-cultural complex in "historical societies." "Literary culture" is another component, but is less important to anthropologists than to historians of religion.

Tambiah did not entirely disregard the notion of "levels." He recognized "interpretational levels" of scientific inquiry; but thought that these should not be confused with the historic componential "levels" which properly concern anthropologists and historians. On the other hand, the general notion of empirical "levels" is problematic, particularly the anthropological distinctions between the literary "higher-level" religion and the popular "lower-level" religion, because the notion itself has proven "frequently inapplicable to the anthropologist's field data and experience." He preferred the notion of integrated "networks" of organization and communication which more usefully serves a scientific or socio-anthropological representation of the complexity of the historic religions. For the ideological, ritual, hierarchical and other networks comprise "continuities" which have been sustained throughout all the transformational changes which serially punctuated their temporal developments. The religions have been "traditions-in-transformation." Hence, their scientific explanation depends on more than the construction of static structural dualities in accordance with the Redfield-Marriott paradigm, and indicates an wholistic approach to the totality of their networks using synchronic and diachronic interpretational categories.

Tambiah accordingly heavily emphasized the important historical dimension in the anthropologist's investigation of currently-existing "traditional" religions. He explained, in World Conqueror and World Renouncer (1976:1-2), that there is an essential "historical dimension" in the anthropologist's scientific study of religious belief-systems tantamount to an anthropo-historical viewpoint or an "historical contextualization" of the socio-anthropological data. The anthropologist faces, for example, "certain problems of contextualization and delimitation in dealing with . . . ritual complexes." This "contextualization" is apparently socio-cultural and historical and implies that Buddhist rites, along with the institution of Buddhist monkhood, and all of their connected religious forms and expressions in the religion of the typical Buddhist village today, have a wider generality in time and space reaching back through the total history of Buddhist developments to its origins in ancient India. There is, in other words, a space-time setting which comprises the "immense [historical] backdrop to the anthropologist's stage" and necessarily shapes the anthropologist's understanding and representation of a religion.

Tambiah (1970:42) clearly saw the truth and relevance of the historical considerations for his own exposition of the religion of Thailand. "The requirements of my exposition" of the religion, he wrote, "are three dimensional: to present the religion as a synchronic, ordered scheme of collective representations; . . . to demonstrate how the system of religious categories is woven into the institutional context and social structure of the contemporary villagers; and . . . to relate the same system to the grand Buddhist literary and historical tradition." He believed that, in order to meet the last of these "requirements," any anthropologist of religions in Buddhist South Asia would have to "find a new way of relating the past to the present." He also indicated this "new way" in his major study of Thai Buddhism (1976:75-76) as "the position and the perspective" of Mus' original representation of the integrational processes joining "great traditions" with local cults. Mus had recognized the relevance of these processes for explaining the origins of Buddhism in India, its earliest connections with national polity in India, and the subsequent spread of "Buddhism and kingship from India to Srī Laṅka and from there to the Thai kingdoms."

Tambiah perceived his socio-historical "new way" in the interpretation of Buddhism in Thailand as his part in "undertaking the grand task of reviewing the spread of Buddhism from various parts of India to various parts of Southeast Asia." He admitted that his contribution to the larger historiographical enterprise would be unavoidably limited to only one of the significant historical dimensions of the Buddhist socio-culture namely its religious totality, specifically the ritual system viewed as a "basic religious pattern" which has been perpetuated throughout all the phases of India's religious development from its prehistoric aboriginal beginnings and on through its brahmanical, upanishadic, and Buddhist phases in ancient India down to present times. But the historical backdrop of the total system of "basic patterns" is the series of its morphological transformations wrought by processes and events initially arising out of the encounter of the primary tradition with regionally located traditions. In regard to contemporary Theravāda Buddhism, the historical backdrop comprises its serial transformations following upon its importation into South Asia and its encounter with pre-Buddhist aboriginal religions and long-standing brahmanical and Mahāyāna Buddhist religions in South Asia and recently impacting western socio-cultural forces.

B. Supernaturalism in Thai Theravāda Buddhism

In a review of Melford E. Spiro's principal works on Burmese religion, Richard Gombrich (1972:483, n.1.) compared him with S.J. Tambiah and remarked that, in Buddhism and Society (1971), Spiro had wrongly judged Tambiah's Buddhism and the Spirit Cults in North-east Thailand (1970) by overlooking supernaturalism in Thai Buddhism and the essential role of "canonical Buddhism" in the religion of the typical Thai villager. Gombrich also noted that Tambiah had misrepresented Spiro's account of Burmese supernaturalism by omitting references to Spiro's elucidation of the intimate relationship of supernaturalism and Buddhism in the religious beliefs and practices of Burma's Buddhist population. Gombrich thought that both scholars misrepresented each other's works "partly because of misunderstanding of each other's methodological approaches." It is apparent that Spiro explicitly represented that intimate relationship in Chapter Fourteen of Burmese Supernaturalism; and that Tambiah discussed the Buddhist elements and features of the spirit-cults of rural Thailand in his study in Buddhism

and the Spirit Cults in North-east Thailand.[6] In this
latter work, Tambiah followed the lead of Ames, Spiro,
and other contemporary social scientists on South and
Southeast Asian religions by connecting supernaturalism
with the "Little Tradition" of Thailand's socio-culture,
and Buddhism with its "Great Tradition," and by
focussing his primary anthropological interest on the
"Little Tradition" supernaturalism. But since six or
seven years passed between his presentation on Thai
supernaturalism and Thai Buddhism the two works on
Buddhism and the Spirit Cults (1970) and World Conqueror
and World Renouncer (1976) reflect his academic career
in the socio-scientific study of religions in South and
Southeast Asia and the course of a discipline which
began with the scientific expeditions into the "Hindu"
field of South Asian religions by Robert Redfield and
his associates in the Chicago School, proceeded into the
Buddhist South Asian field and its interpretational
adaptations of Redfield's socio-cultural paradigm, and
culminated in the socio-historical paradigm envisaged by
Tambiah for the scientific explanation of religions in
Buddhist South Asia.

Tambiah pointed out in Buddhism and the Spirit
Cults of North-east Thailand (1970) that Buddhism is a
component of Thai rural-village religion, not a feature
of it. But in World Conqueror and World Renouncer
(1976) he admitted that "Little Tradition" religious
systems which scholars assume to be "non-Buddhist"
comprise instead lower-level popular and folk forms of
Thailand's "Great Tradition" Buddhist metasystem. In
other words, all of the religious systems of Thailand
which social scientists have conceptually differentiated
actually derive from, belong to, and function within the
one Buddhist tradition. This implies much more than
supposing they share in its "Buddhist ethos."

In his earlier work, Tambiah (1970:1-3) admitted that Buddhism is "an integral feature" of Thai village religion inasmuch as the religious beliefs and practices of Buddhist monks residing in the villages include features belonging to the larger synchronic system of Thai "village religion." He attempted to illustrate this structural interconnection within the rural-village religious system specifically in regard to its ritual complex which reflects four distinguishable religions: theistic Buddhism, canonical Buddhism, "the cult of malevolent spirits," and "the cult of guardian spirits and deities of the village." Tambiah also attempted to ascertain the full spacial and temporal "projections" of these component systems by analyzing the structures of each and tracing back the sequences of their earlier forms and roots in the Buddhism and the non-Buddhism of Buddhist South Asia and ancient mainland India. He believed that the structural analyses could be extended to the larger network of functional and cultural interlinkages connecting Thailand's village-religion as a whole with its urban counterparts and with the corresponding historic networks in the neighbouring Theravāda Buddhist countries of Burma, Laos, Cambodia and Ceylon showing a shared framework of religious meaning and identity, "a synchronic ordered scheme of [component religious] representations" woven into "the institutional context," temporal relation to "the grand literary historical tradition" of Theravāda Buddhism linking present-day mainland Southeast Asia with ancient mainland India.

Tambiah (1970:2-5) also recognized his four conceptually distinguished different religious traditions as being dimensions to the "single total field" of "village religion." He understood that it is this "single total field" that the anthropologist interested in religion properly tries to interpret and explain within the parameters of his scientific discipline. Moreover, the total-field of Thai-village religion is amenable to a threefold structural and historical interpretation through: (i), an elucidation of its integral components, that is, of its ideology, its rituals, its officiants, its "cults" of supernaturalistic Buddhism, animism, and the "guardian spirits," and "canonical Buddhism"; (ii) a systematic "ordering" of "the contrastive features" of the four "cults" (including "canonical Buddhism") which could portray them as "collective representations" of the structural features of the village-religion in contrastive relational terms of "opposition, complementarity, linkage, and hierarchy"; and (iii) the interpretation of its complexity as an historical pattern comprising persistent "continuities" and serial "transformations" punctuating its progression through space and time. He concluded that the religion of the typical present-day Thai-village community displays "the present contemporary modes" of the "contrapuntal theme" of "continuity through transformation." The present complexity, accordingly, demonstrates "how the past lives in the present" and also how "the present can . . be seen as a transformation of the past."

It is apparent, in this regard, that Tambiah's interpretation melded the earlier forms with the contemporary forms of the religion, the spacial with the temporal transformations, and the structural-functional and socio-historical perspectives on religion in rural Thailand. Behind it was his most significant empirical observation and contribution to the historical study of religions that any contemporary "traditional" socio-culture, such as the religious system of a typical Thai village, is the present summation of its total history.

Accordingly a scientifically sound characterization and explanation of such a "traditional religion" demands a structural-historical approach, because a purely "academic" historical approach would misrepresent the religion as though it was a static entity lacking transitional characteristics due to transformational influences in its socio-cultural environment, and a structuralist approach alone would also be static and a-historical on account of excluding perceptions of the dynamic influences of its socio-cultural environment upon its structural organization. A "structural-historical" or a "socio-structural-historical" or a "socio-historical" approach could do justice to the transformations and the continuities which have constituted its present historic complexity.

This does not imply that Tambiah conceived the "socio-historical approach" as a displacement of, or even as a continuative extension of, the "academic historical approach." He thought of it instead as a supportive informational adjunct to the "classical approach" in the history of religions. There is a priorization in the scientific study of religions which is structuralist first, functionalist second, and historical third. The structuralist priorization was indicated by Tambiah in a statement of the general objective of his exploration of the Thai religion: to shed light on the intimate interrelation between its "village religion" and "the social structure and institutional environment of the people who practice the religion." It was also affirmed by his belief that the structural-functional characterization of such a socio-cultural totality constitutes the anthropologist's distinctive contribution to the scientific or academic study of religion by virtue of his discipline's approach and method.

But he also rejected an exclusive "structuralist-functionalist" approach and a "purely historical" approach. The one is too "static and a-historical." The other is too abstract and antiquarian in regard to its historical interpretation of the tradition in terms of the genesis and growth of its primal doctrinal and institutional features. There can be a "structural-historical approach" or a socio-historical approach which combines the sociologist's scientific interest in the contemporary forms of "traditional" religions with the academic historian's interest in them as the present outcome of their earlier formations. Analyses of the traditional religion of contemporary Thailand disclose the factors and conditions behind its genesis and historic development. But these are deductively ascertainable socio-cultural conditions and transformational forces whose sequential collectivity empirically comprises the expanded "history" of the religion of Thailand from early to modern times.

C. Thai Buddhism's Rural and Urban Contexts

In the socio-anthropology of folk-religion, Tambiah's distinctive contribution lies in his structuralistic exposition of the interrelations of Buddhism and folk-religion in the religion of rural Thailand's Buddhist peasants. His analysis of the ritual-component of the village-religion complex displayed four distinguishable subsystems of which two are "Buddhist" and two are "non-Buddhist." But while distinguishing "the Buddhist ritual" or public rites performed by monks, the kwan rites or domestic rituals performed by them for households, kin, and neighbours, the rites reflecting a "cult of guardian spirits," and "rites [of appeasement] addressed to malevolent spirits," Tambiah also considered whether or not these could be integratively represented either as: (i) an "hierarchy" of expanding units emerging developmentally out of each other; or (ii) a succession of temporal accretions; or (iii) as "contrastive features" within the poly-dimensional ritual-organization of the Buddhist metasystem of Thailand's peasant-folk.

Tambiah's diagrammatic representation of the ritual-system (1970:338, figure 5) indicates his adoption of the third of the representational alternatives. But his sole representation of the ritual complex, without inclusion of the cosmological, mythic, theistic, institutional, and other componential facets of rural Thai Buddhism, limited its scientific value. Nor was this deficiency compensated in his later major work on Thai Buddhism and national polity even though its perspective embraced both the urban and the rural arenas of Thai Buddhism. The separation of the two religious complexes in Tambiah's major works prevented the question and its answer of whether or not, or to what extent, the Thai-village folk-religion is a localized version of a general Buddhism of Thailand.

On the other hand, his exploration of the village-religion was methodologically guided by the Redfield-Marriott dichotomy whose conceptual and theoretical frameworks seemed interpretively relevant in regard to the interactions and impingements of the "Great Tradition" of Theravāda Buddhism on the "Little Tradition" religion of rural Thailand's peasant-folk. His scientific interpretation of the religion practiced in the northeast Thai village of Baan Phraan Muan was an attempt at resolving the structuralist problem of whether or not the connection of its religion with Thai Buddhism is an external one tied to certain specific communicational linkages, or is an intrinsic relation due to the historical development of Thai Buddhism within the pre-Buddhist traditional religion of that

village and the assimilation of the primal religion with
the Buddhist "Great Tradition" in Thailand. The
indications are that Tambiah leaned toward the latter
viewpoint which would have represented the village
religion as a specific local mode of a syncretic
Theravāda Buddhist religion generally espoused by
Thailand's Buddhist-majority population. The urban
Buddhism in Thailand also reflects similar assimilations
between local and imported forms of pre-Buddhist and
Buddhist religion in Thailand.

Tambiah specifically indicated this assimilation
between two components of "classical Buddhism" presented
in "Buddhist literary works," namely: the Buddhist
cosmology which is "ritually enacted in village
religion," and "Buddhist monasticism" which is
"classically conceived" in the Pali texts and is
"institutionalized in contemporary village life."
Moreover, he drew from the "classical Buddhist
literature" his "internal differentiation" of the
"Buddhist" and the "non-Buddhist" components of the
Thai-village religion. The field-data, garnered from
observations of the practice of Buddhism among village-
residing monks and peasants, presumably provided his
external differentiation of the components.

The textually-grounded internal differentiation did
not resolve the problem of contradictory "levels" which
the Redfieldian synchronic and diachronic categories
imposed on socio-anthropological interpretations of the
religion, or which Tambiah, following Dumont and Pocock,
had criticized. Nevertheless, the structuralist
distinctions which the Redfieldian "Great
Tradition/Little Tradition" dichotomy had furnished for
the interpretation of religions in South Asia guided
Tambiah's understanding of the religion. He supported
Obeyesekere and his contemporaries by drawing attention

to the underlying unity of the composite religion espoused by the folk-majority of Buddhists in South and Southeast Asia. He agreed that the peasant-folk in Buddhist South Asia espouse one religion only and have traditionally identified this with Theravāda Buddhism although in fact it comprises conceptually distinguishable "Buddhist" and "non-Buddhist" components, features, elements, and traits indicating that it is a hybrid or "secondary" religious system.

His adoption of their views, however, involved the same pitfalls which dogged the Redfieldian sociological studies of the religions throughout the nineteen-sixties and seventies. For the supposition of the unity of the religions and the presentation of a plurality of religions in the religions of South Asia's Theravāda Buddhists seem contradictory. But the distinction had sound empirical bases in regard to a pluralistic "historic" Buddhism and a monolithic "canonical" Buddhism in South Asia. Tambiah evidently attempted to explain scientifically the factual contradiction between the canonical Buddhism of the monks and the sacred texts and the popular Buddhism practiced in Thailand's villages, towns, and cities along lines of a historical explanation of Thai-village Buddhism in terms of the continuity of its core components and the transformations of its forms when the pre-Buddhist and imported Buddhist traditions became syncretically melded and reshaped during each of its subsequent centuries.

In this connection, the article on "The Persistence and Transformation of Tradition in Southeast Asia, with special reference to Thailand" (1973) is a landmark exposition of Tambiah's theoretical and methodological approaches to a socio-history of religions in Thailand, particularly in reference to Theravāda Buddhism. Its primary and fundamental assumption is that the character of Theravāda Buddhism is determined by the dynamic socio-cultural conditions and forces prevailing at each juncture and phase of its history. Throughout each of its temporal phases a "dynamic of change" is operative yet "the continuities of the past" in that religion remain integrally connected with the "transformations of the present." This dynamic integration of "continuity" and "transformational change" is generally illustrated by the history of Theravāda Buddhism and is singularly illustrated by the union of Buddhism with national polity from Aśokan to modern times.

In this demonstration, Tambiah defined Redfield's concept of "tradition" as "some kind of collective heritage which, contrary to assumptions by politicians, historians of religion, sociologists, scholars, and others, has not been transmitted relatively unchanged from the past." Instead, the tradition has been affected by "dialectical tensions" of "communication and interchange" between "the continuities" of its past and the adjustive acculturations or "transformations" which unfolded its complexity from early times down to the present. Moreover, the "dialectical tensions" which have punctuated the historic course of the canonical textual tradition of Buddhism are different from those which are behind the "historical Buddhism" from its beginnings and throughout its "later developments" and "accretions notably from the time of the Emperor Aśoka onwards."[7] Hence, the more recent changes in contemporary Theravāda Buddhism through the forces and influences of its "politicization and socialization" are interpretable as specific occasions of more general changes which have shaped the history of Theravāda Buddhism since the early centuries of its expansion in Buddhist South Asia.[8]

Like Obeyesekere, Tambiah assumed that Theravāda
Buddhism is "a common religion" for the Theravāda
Buddhist countries of South and Southeast Asia
interlinking them religiously through a network of
shared "communication and interchange . . . on religious
matters." This general Theravāda Buddhism has
contrasting national and regional forms in each
Theravāda Buddhist country in which it is "officially
supported." This is because each regional Theravāda
Buddhism has been differently shaped by its respective
socio-cultural environment. There is a counterpart to
this regional environmental factor behind the forms of
Buddhism in each village, town, and city in Buddhist
South Asia. But Tambiah did not explore all these
connections, but only the developing patterns of
regional Buddhistic development and particularly the
"different proportions" of "politics and religion"
producing "different compounds" of Theravāda Buddhism in
each of the principal Theravāda Buddhist countries of
South and Southeast Asia. He interpreted these as
features of their respective histories showing
"temporary crystallizations" constituted by "a limited
set of possibilities" for change, persisting for limited
times, and related to the "deeper underlying and
persisting set of dialectical tensions stemming from the
historical relationship between Buddhism and polity from
the Aśokan era in India, and subsequently from the
various Buddhist kingdoms of South and Southeast Asia."[9]
The most important conclusion drawn from this
specific relation of Buddhism and politics is that
contemporary Buddhism in South Asia is the totality and
present summation of its preceding forms, conditions and
changes. Accordingly, its explanation by social
scientists, as well as by historians of religions,
requires consideration of the development of its

interior or structural patterns as well as of its
exterior elitist, urban, rural, and peasant forms.
Tambiah conceived this as an overview of all the forms
through which Theravāda Buddhism moved historically
through the morphological changes superimposed upon its
unchanging intrinsic identity. For throughout the
centuries there has never been lost an "active
consciousness of [Buddhism's] historical continuity."
This continuity was sometimes "alleged, accentuated, and
burgeoned" during particularly acute social and
political conditions, or "suffered eclipses and amnesias
during various periods of decline." Nevertheless,
especially "at times of resurgence and expansion, old
literary texts and mythologies . . . provided . . .
models for revival and lent an air of authenticity to
the claim of continuity." Moreover, "certain tradition-
based dialectical themes relating to politics and
religion "revived in" new situations generated by
contacts with "other" cultures and traditions. These
"vitally affected" the "sacred cultural traditions,"
ideologically, such as through reinterpretations of
canonical texts, and institutionally, such as through
changing roles of the Buddhist monks and their
monasteries. This reinterpretive dialectic is reflected
most recently in Buddhadasa's modernistic conception of
the Buddhist monastic vocation, and through "the various
community development and 'missionizing' programs
variously called Dhammathud, Dhammacarika, and
Dhammapatana which changed "the infrastructural bases"
of the Saṅgha's traditional "role as an educational
network."[10]

Tambiah perceived these effects of the "Western
impact" on the Buddhist traditions in Southeast Asia as
only the most recent in the long chain of
transformations effected in the sacred traditions of

"smaller in-between societies" of South and Southeast
Asia which had been subjected in the past to "waves of
conquest and new influences" from India and China.
These changes included their stratified "archeological
layerings" and accretions of Indian, Chinese, and
Western "structural and dialectical orientations" drawn
from the "wider frame" of their socio-historical
reference, as well as the "important peculiarities and
distinctive features" of their historic regional
actualizations in the Theravāda Buddhist countries of
South and Southeast Asia as illustrated by the Buddhism
of Thailand.

D. The Historical Reconstruction of the Buddhist Social Reality in Thailand

While the concern behind Tambiah's earlier work was
the temporal infusions of rural Thailand's aboriginal
and pre-Buddhist supernaturalism with Buddhist
supernaturalism, the concern behind his later work was
the extensive urban and rural ramifications of
contemporary Thailand's politicized Theravāda Buddhism
having historic roots in the Asokan period of Buddhist
India. His study of Thai Buddhism and national polity
in World Conqueror and World Renouncer (1976) fulfilled
a "promise" that he would complement his "microscopic"
study of "the great tradition of Buddhism" and its
refraction in "the microcosm of village life" by "a
macroscopic study of the Thai-Buddhist connection with
Thai society as a whole." This would be examined in the
light of its Asokan political-Buddhist backdrop but
would follow its temporal trajectory in South and
Southeast Asia from the third century B.C. down to the
nineteenth century when it "collided with the West and
launched on modernization" with its western
"developments and structures."11

Tambiah (1976:5) also conceived his project on Thai Buddhism as "a panoramic and telescopic overview of contemporary Thai society" from the perspective of Buddhism. But it transpired into a sophisticated insight into "the internal organization and economic bases of Thai Buddhism" disclosed by its "urban monasteries and urban religion" but informed by an historical perspective. Nevertheless, he held the opinion that "a holistic conception of Buddhist polity in nineteenth-century and twentieth-century Thai society" cannot be realized without an ascertainment of "the central conception between Buddhism and polity predicated in early Buddhism."

This, however, "presupposes a retrospective historical view of an intellectual process" or the retracing of "a regressive historical passage" by which contemporary Thailand's Buddhist polity is interpretively related through each of its preceding phases back to its beginning time. Tambiah presupposed that, by "following the [historical] projectory from contemporary Thailand to early Indian Buddhism" he could reconstruct an empirically valid general history of Thai Buddhism set within the political history of Thailand. This retrospective historical method is tantamount to the recollection of the series of transformations which have occurred within and between the "recurrent structures" or "continuities" of Thai Buddhism. Moreover, by pursuing the reconstructive process within each of the principal organizations of Thai Buddhism- its polity, economics, social institutions, culture, and religion - an historical reconstruction of the total Thai-Buddhist socio-culture could be effected in systematic terms.

This envisaged historical retrospection in his sociology of Thailand accordingly shaped Tambiah's arrangement of <u>World Conqueror and World Renouncer</u>. He planned it as a two-part study providing historical and structural representations of "early Buddhism in India" in its first part, and "the nexus among religion, saṅgha and polity in contemporary Thailand" in its second part. Moreover, the first or structural-historical part, was to be extruded from "the documentation of its [i.e. <u>early Buddhism's</u>] tenets, world image, and ideas of salvation and societal order" for the purpose of showing its divergences from the brahmanical forms of religion in ancient India. These forms specifically included the brahmanical court-religion which supplied the earliest Buddhist conceptions of kingship and polity which became "legendarily realized in the epochal reign of Emperor Asoka" and provided the primal model and precedent "for some of the emergent polities of South and Southeast Asia." Tambiah also intended the first part to be an expanded preface for or introduction to the second part. His objective for this part was an "in-depth study" of the ideological premisses, the organizational structure, and the social expressions of the political Theravada Buddhism of Thailand ascertained through empirical "field-studies" of the interrelation of Buddhism and Thai national polity in contemporary Thailand.

Both of the parts clearly show that Tambiah adopted the current academic history of Buddhism in Thailand and the rest of Buddhist South Asia and drew from its textual historiographical data, rather than his empirical field-data, the main substance of his interpretational conclusions. This preference restricted his socio-historical perspective on Theravāda Buddhism to its elitist expressions and the crucial relation of its principal institution, the Sangha, to the Buddhist monarchy in the Thai national polity. This elitism accordingly distorted his empirical representation of the total social reality of Thai Buddhism. Even his arbitrary selection of minor pieces of early Buddhist dharmaśāstra such as the Aggaṇṇa Suttānta (1976:9-18) for reconstructing the early Buddhist version of society and kingship misled his interpretation of the Buddhist "social gospel." He allowed the Buddhist literary tradition as a whole to predetermine what could legitimately be counted as "Buddhist" or else as "non-Buddhist" in the religion of Thailand's Buddhists and prevented an authentic historical representation of Thai Buddhism's syncretical history.

Tambiah, nonetheless, deserves the most credit for recognizing explicitly the complex socio-cultural context within which the "total phenomenon of Theravāda Buddhism" has been historically defined. He saw it, in that context, as being more than an ideology enshrined in the institutional organization and religious practices of the Saṅgha. Tambiah (1976:35) made this the central posit of his "manifesto" which he based on a quotation by Paul Mus (1964:25) that: "Buddhism in its full historical significance, is not just a psychological and somewhat paradoxical revelation, curiously developing into a world religion . . . . In fact, it proved a social as well as a moral revolution. It had enough practical efficacity not only to renovate for a period of several centuries the style and sense of life in India, but to expand all over Central, Eastern and Southeastern Asia."

In his essay on Thai Buddhism and national polity Tambiah stated the timeliness of a new critical re-assessment of the "protagonist mythologization" of the emperor Aśoka presented in the Sinhalese chronicles on account of its misleading views on Buddhist kingship and polity based on the earlier royal mythologization of the

<u>Buddha</u> in the Nikāyas. He recognized that the relation of Buddhist kingship and national polity in Thailand had been highly complex, according to the historical study by Gordon Luce (1969: Vol.I) on the transitions of the Buddhist tradition in Thailand during the tenth and eleventh centuries of pre-Aniruddha and Aniruddha Pagan when a "widespread paganism" peacefully coexisted along with "Buddhism and Vaisnavism in court circles." This was followed in the eleventh-century Aniruddha period (c.1044-1077 A.D.) by the Buddhist ascendancy "in the religio-political field" and the final "triumph" of Theravāda Buddhism through the importation of the full <u>Tripitaka</u> from Ceylon (c.1075 A.D.).

Tambiah called into question several significant details in Luce's representation of the syncretic pluralism of the earlier and later Thai Buddhism. Luce and other scholars had assumed that several historically and organizationally distinct yet contemporaneous ritual systems functioned separately within the same ritual space. He supposed that the ritual-system served by the Buddhist monks is "Buddhism," and the ritual-system served by the "Vaisnava priests" is Vaisnavism. In effect, this set <u>two</u> distinct traditions within the Pagan Court-religion and overlooked any syncretizing processes which might have produced a hybrid hinduistic royal Buddhism of Pagan contrasting with other contemporaneous heterogenetic counterparts within the general Buddhism of eleventh-century Thailand. For the pragmatical unity of the ritual ministrations of the <u>bhikkhu</u> and the <u>brahman</u> in the Pagan royal court appears to mirror the popular religion of the period showing Buddhism reconciled with the "widespread paganism" such as Luce observed in the Buddhistic religion of Pre-Aniruddha Pagan. In other words, any ideological and institutional differences which might have visibly distinguished the two religions in the ancient past must have become dissolved prior to the emergence of the Buddhaized-Brāhmanism or Brāhmanical-Buddhism of the Pagan Court and the syncretic versions of "popular Buddhism" in urban and rural Thailand.

Nevertheless, despite his own critique of Luce's dichotomization of the Pagan religion, and his counter-hypothesis on the "essential and integral relationship between Buddhism and Brāhmanism" in the court-religion of Pagan, Tambiah did not adumbrate a syncretistic history of Buddhism in Thailand. Instead, Tambiah (1976:83-84) submitted a limited modification of Luce's historical "thesis" concerning the Buddhist "transformation of the brahmanical formula" of kingship effecting a "change from the narrow doctrine of rājadharma (in which the brāhman sanctifies kingship) to the larger conception of dharmarāja (wherein the king is the wielder of this-worldly dharma and the maintainer of society, in which brāhmans serve as subordinate functionaries, and wherein he [i.e. the king] has the duty of protecting and tending the members of the saṅgha as seekers of the higher truth." He understood that, since "under the aegis of kingship, both bhikkhu and brāhman . . . stand to each other in a complementary relation," this presupposes a structural as well as an institutional framework in which earlier historical distinctions had become syncretically dissolved into the complex metasystem of "historic Buddhism" in Thailand.

This hypothesis is not intended to read like another version of the old bi-level socio-historical theory of an historically intact Buddhism having survived its superimposition upon a pre-Buddhist supernaturalistic substratum. The royal Buddhism of Pagan admittedly seems to illustrate this duality of a saṅghika-Buddhism at its upper level and the sectarian

Vaiṣṇava-Brāhmanism as its lower level. The popular Buddhism of this period and later similarly reflects a bi-level system comprising "Theravāda Buddhism" as its superstructure and aboriginal paganism as its substratum. But the point which Wilhelm Geiger (1960:176) made concerning the Mahāvaṁsa is applicable to that Buddhism also and throughout South Asia because it "shows us how fallacious it is entirely to separate Buddhism from Brāhmanism" either in its later periods or in medieval Buddhist Asia.

Tambiah reflected Geiger's point through a structural representation of the total religious system in Thailand which displays his perceptive awareness of the principle that changes in any one component are reciprocated throughout the total metasystem beginning with the most proximate and ending with the most peripheral, components. It also reflected his rejection of "that kind of developmental thesis" that Buddhism began with "the purely 'religious' doctrines of a charismatic leader as the founder of a sect of salvation-seekers" before becoming evolved into a universal religion, or began solely as "a salvation quest for the virtuosi." Instead, it must have developed into a complex religious system through an historic intertwining of diverse religious traditions.

Tambiah's sense of Buddhism's multiple development was continued in his reflections upon the local, regional and national forms of Buddhism's ideological, ritual, political, institutional, and other historic expressions which indicate a profounder view of the complexity of Theravāda Buddhism's history in South Asia than Hermann Oldenburg presented in his textually-oriented nineteenth-century classic study of Theravāda Buddhism. Tambiah's eclectic perspective incorporated Buddhism's extensive pagan cultism with its pantheon of

Hinduistic deities, spirits, heroes, and demons modelled on the current brahmanical cosmology and cosmogony, constellated around the grandiose figure of the divine Buddha, and interpreted by the textual theistic imagery of primitive Buddhism. His insights on the integrative dynamics by which indigenous and the imported religious elements became melded into the complexity of its regional and national Buddhisms, particularly in regard to the syncretic history of Buddhism and the "spirit cults" in Thailand, justify the estimation by Martin Barber and Victor King (1973) that his work "is a fine example of what Evans-Pritchard, Levi-Strauss and others have been stressing on the importance of history for social anthropologists."[11] Barber and King particularly applauded his effective use of "historical techniques" around the concepts of "continuity" and "transformation."

Frank Reynolds (1978:258-268) appreciated his interpretational applications of Thai buddhological and historical information to the present-day Thai religion so that it could be seen as the most recent Thai Buddhism and as an illustration of the outcome of dialectical ambiguities, tensions and paradoxes which shaped the development of Buddhism throughout Buddhist South Asia. His appreciation of Tambiah's socio-history of Thai religion had one reservation, that he overlooked "the dynamic interaction and interpenetration" which certainly took place "between the dominant Theravāda tradition and competing forces associated with various Mahāyāna traditions, with messianic strands within the Theravāda community itself, and with the indigenous cadastral patterns that were never fully integrated into the system." But Tambiah did not present an analysis of the total religious system in Thailand embracing all of its component features; instead, he outlined a concentric-circular scheme of configuration for the ritual-system only although he thought that the scheme would demonstrate the applicability of his technique for the systematic representation and interpretation of the mythological, cosmological, hierarchical, and other systemic components of the total religious system.

Tambiah also incorporated peripheral religious systems into his survey of Thai Buddhism. He recognized these as being "tolerated" by the Buddhist leaderships on account of their complementative religious functions. He perceived their contributions to Buddhist historical development as having parallels in the historic growth of Hinduism through its expansive incorporation of major and minor regional and local religious systems which had different origins at different times and in different places of India yet also retained a measure of independent continuance outside of the gargantuan Hindu metasystem.

Tambiah's contributions toward a polydimensional historical reconstruction of Buddhism in South and Southeast Asia could have substantially advanced Mus' originative reconstructionist-history of India's ancient religions by displaying Buddhism as a complex socio-culture having multiple socio-cultural strata rather than historically distinct, contemporaneous "upper level" and "lower level" traditions. But, insofar as Tambiah was willing to preserve the notion of "levels," he did so with the qualification that these should not be interpreted in static, abstract, and atomic terms, but as "sets of relations" forming "dynamic structures" which reflect "textual and social realities" which cumulatively developed through "shifts in principles and ideas . . . over vast periods of time." He also perceived that the socio-cultural forces, conditions and processes behind the cumulative developments could be incorporated into a reconstructed "history" of Buddhism in South Asia comprising its elitist, popular and folk expressions and its dynamically integrated ideological, ritual, and institutional, etc., infrastructures. In this light, Reynold's concern about Tambiah's omission of the exterior indigenous religious systems from his wholistic representation of the Thai religion is reduced to the central issue of the requisite scope of a socio-history of Theravāda Buddhism accounting for the total social fact in each of its geographical regions, in all of its developmental phases, and at all of the cultural levels indicated by the elite and popular religious beliefs, practices, and institutions of South Asia's Theravāda Buddhists.

E. The Syncretic Complexity of Thai Buddhism

The published works by B.J. Terwiel and A. Thomas Kirsch on Thai Buddhism reflect the consummation of the Redfieldian sociological research on Buddhism during the nineteen-sixties and seventies. This is because both scholars prefaced their publications by reviews of the scientific field in which their own researches on Thai Buddhism had been conducted, and each presented his work as overcoming the pitfalls of earlier researches, and advancing or fulfilling their contributions to scholarship on religions in Buddhist South Asia.

B.J. Terwiel (1975:391-393) divided the sociological field into the two "camps" of the structuralists and the historians, into the two "groups" of the "syncretists" and "the multiple layer groups," and their works into six interpretational "approaches." He distinguished in their works: (1) statements to the effect that Theravāda Buddhists are syncretistic and pluralistic in their religious beliefs, and adhere to several strands of religion including "non-Buddhist beliefs" as well as "other-worldly Buddhism";[12] (2)

statements implying that South Asian Buddhists adhere to
a syncretistic blend of religious traditions of which
their "Buddhist" and "non-Buddhist" beliefs and
practices are indistinguishable from each other;[13] (3)
statements indicating that Buddhists in Southeast Asia
practice "complementary subtypes of religion" by using
Buddhism for meeting concerns about their future life
and "local religious beliefs" for dealing with "the
magical side of everyday life";[14] (4) statements that
Buddhists in Southeast Asia have contradictory or
"incompatible and opposed" animistic and Buddhist
religious orientations;[15] (5) statements that Buddhists
adhere to "three separate traditions of Buddhism,
Brahmanism, and Supernaturalism;[16] and (6) statements
that Buddhists of South and Southeast Asia have their
"religious field" dominated by "four major cults."[17]
Among these, the only "consensus" that Terwiel found
among the several representatives of these approaches
appeared to be their "general agreement . . . with
regard to the opinion that, next to the Buddhist faith,
there can be found in Theravāda Buddhist countries one
or more layers of non-Buddhist religion." He otherwise
noted the wide disagreements among them concerning "the
number of strata that can be recognized, . . . their
interrelations,. and . . . the value of distinguishing
between these layers." Terwiel did not attempt to
resolve the disagreements; instead, he decided to apply
investigative procedures which could indicate which of
the six scientific "approaches" adopted by the
"syncretists" and the "multiple layer group" could best
serve a scientific characterization and explanation of
the religious complex in contemporary Thailand.[18]

 For this purpose, he presupposed the current
sociological distinction between the "Buddhist" and the
"non-Buddhist" components of the Thai religion. He

assumed, also, that the sociologist's distinctive
scientific task is to ascertain, through "in-depth
interviews" and other sociological methods, "the
relation between Buddhism and non-Buddhist practices" in
Thai-village religion.[19] He was not apparently aware of
the problematic criteria governing the sociological
distinctions between the "Buddhist" and "non-Buddhist"
forms of the traditional religion in Thailand. He
simply assumed that Buddha-images and any conduct which
is "in perfect accordance with the rules of the
Patimokkha" are "unequivocally Buddhist," that there are
also beliefs and practices traditionally adopted by
Thailand's peasant-farmers which are "generally known as
Buddhist," and there is a visible remainder which are
"interpreted in terms of animism" although they "appear
to be fully incorporated into the farmer's religion."

Terwiel drew these strands together into the
picture of a magico-animistic system of rituals and
beliefs sanctioned and sanctified by Buddhism,
supplemented by Buddhist elements, presided over by non-
participating Buddhist monks, and sacralized by monks
chanting "in loud and clear voices a certain number of
Pali texts" while holding "a cotton thread" at chest
level "connected to a bowl of water and to a Buddha
image." But his conception of the system as being
neither fully within the conspectus of Buddhism nor yet
entirely outside of it, that is "non-Buddhist", is
highly problematic. Moreover, the real religion which
he found and described does not empirically indicate a
dualistic "Buddhist/non-Buddhist" interpretation but a
syncretistically complex folk-Buddhism in which Buddhist
components of foreign origin and local animistic beliefs
and practices have long become syncretically integrated.

Nevertheless, whereas the majority of Terwiel's
professional contemporaries in the sociology of South

and Southeast Asian religions focussed their interpretation upon their conceptual differentiations of the "Buddhist" and the "non-Buddhist" levels or strata in the Thai religion, Terwiel focussed his interest upon behavioural distinctions. He interpreted these psychologistically as reflections of the "different levels of awareness" which the researcher could link with underlying animistic, supernaturalistic and Buddhist "principles" of which "the actors" might be unaware. For example, he perceived the support given by monks to the popular folk rituals as unwitting contradictions of their Buddhist principles indicating the weakening impact of "the historical Great Tradition" of Theravāda Buddhism upon "religious life in isolated rural monasteries" and the present need for belated reaffirmative Buddhist reforms.

On the other hand, Terwiel recognized the intermingling of religion and magic in the current scheme of religious power and merit and their Buddhist sanctification through rites of monastic blessing as a visible indicator of the extensively reticulated network of religious interconnections between clergy and laity making the unified tradition of rural Thailand's Theravāda Buddhism. Citing John Brohm's study in 1963 of "a similar animistic religion in rural Burma," Terwiel drew a contrast between this rural form of Thai Theravāda Buddhism and the "fundamentally different religious orientation" of "the sophisticated urban Buddhist" and "member of the educated elite." But he psychologistically interpreted the contrasts not as the "discrepancy" between two contradictory Buddhisms, but as compartmentalized abstractions between the conceptually-defined canonical Theravāda Buddhism of the urbanite elites, and the pragmatical "animistic Buddhism" of the peasant-majority of Thai Buddhists. He

also recognized an interconnecting third or in-between
Buddhism of "the members of the expanding middle class"
whose religious outlook is simultaneously oriented
toward the contrasting sophisticate and unsophisticate
Buddhisms.[20]

Terwiel particularly contrasted the mental stances
behind the syncretistic religious outlook of the
Buddhist peasant-farmer in rural Thailand on the one
hand and the psychologistically compartmentalized and
abstractly conceived Theravāda Buddhism of Thailand's
urban elites on the other. He did not deduce from these
contrasting psychological orientations the existence of
two substantively real and different religious
traditions, but interpreted them as distinguishable
modes in which the one tradition had been made openly
syncretical by the rural group and
compartmentalistically "bracketed" by the urban group.

Terwiel's distinctions between the "structuralists"
and the "historians" and between the syncretic and
compartmentalized appropriations of Theravāda Buddhism
in Thailand were adopted and expanded in Kirsch's
representation of the Thai religious totality. Like
Terwiel, Kirsch (1977) perceived in the "Thai religious
complexity" a "shared situation" which has counterparts
among "other South and Southeast Asian peoples who
commonly identify themselves as Theravāda Buddhists."
The Theravāda Buddhism of Thailand presents an historic
merging of "once-distinct religious traditions." But
they do not refer to this syncretic outcome as
"Theravāda Buddhism."

Kirsch also observed that a "similar complexity" to
the one which is found in the rural and the urban "Thai
religious situation" can be recognized also in the rural
and urban religious situations of the Sri Lankan, the
Burmese, Cambodian, Laotian, and other Theravāda

Buddhist societies where "elements derived from several historically discrete traditions have combined to form a single distinctive tradition." But whereas Terwiel interpreted this contrastive duality in psychologistical terms of "levels of awareness," Kirsch interpreted it in historical or socio-historical terms of temporal and spacially conditioned mergers. In this respect, his interpretation was more closely aligned with "the historical approach" among "the syncretist group" of sociologists researching on South and Southeast Asian religions.[21]

But Kirsch's major contribution toward an historical understanding of religions in contemporary Buddhist South Asia lies in the importance which he attached to the indivisible social context of the Thai religious complex and its parallels in regional Theravāda Buddhist South Asia.[22] Theravāda Buddhism appears in this contextual light as a variable repeatedly subjected to changing socio-cultural conditions peculiar to each Buddhist society and community which appropriated it. Moreover, since each social context is a "variable," its variations constitute the major determinants behind the successive transformations through which Theravāda Buddhism historically passed in South and Southeast Asia. Furthermore, the specific forms of these Theravāda Buddhist changes have necessarily corresponded to the variant urban, rural, elite, middle-class, peasant-folk, monastic, and lay sectors of its social nexuses.

Kirsch's perception of these historically determinative variables affecting Theravāda Buddhism should have led to an historical conclusion on the diversification of Theravāda Buddhism in Thailand's Buddhist society. But instead of recognizing these diversifications of the religion of Thailand's Theravāda

Buddhists as "higher" and "lower" modes of the same Buddhism, Kirsch separated out "three components in Thai religion" - the "Buddhist," the "Brahmanistic," and the "animistic" - and attempted their explanation in structural-functionalistic terms describing their interrelations within the "perduring pattern" of the Thai religion, including its changes "in recent years."

The interpretational end-result of his variegational representation, however, is unfortunately confusing. He found in the Thai religion "an imported Buddhism encountered by the Thais"; a "Buddhism . . . recognized as the state religion"; the "Theravāda Buddhism" which has "maintained its unity and continuity through a common core of doctrines and rituals sustained by a monastic institution"; the "sophisticated Buddhism" of "a small group of virtuosos and literati"; a popular Buddhism comprising "Buddhist values and beliefs" which have "set the religious context that has shaped the institutional fabric of Thai society" as well as of Thai daily life and attitudes to the everyday world; the "philosophical Buddhism" shown by its postulates and phenomenal and noumenal "perspectives" on "the two levels of reality"; the "abstract Buddhism"; the "formal Buddhism"; and, the "doctrinal Buddhism."[23]

Some of these forms, no doubt, are empirically identical. Yet it cannot be supposed that the Thais have simultaneously practiced nine or less distinguishable Buddhist systems, but only that their one religion has had temporal and regional variants including its animistic mode principally among Thailand's rural peasant-folk, its merit-making mode principally among the laity forming "the mass of Thai Buddhists," the "abstract Buddhism" or "doctrinal Buddhism" of the literati and virtuosos, and the political or "formal mode" of Buddhism behind the royal annual donation of monastic robes or <u>kathin</u> ceremony in which the State Buddhism and the <u>saṅghika</u> Buddhism appear to meet.

But even the highly compartmentalized distinctions which Kirsch (1977:251-260) drew between "folk Brāhmanism," "folk animism," and "folk Buddhism" are not as contrastive as he indicated. Kirsch did not overlook the syncretistical implications of "brahmanistic elements" in the Thai religion which are not "unequivocally identified as Buddhist," and he recognized "the possibility . . . that this Folk Brahmanic complex was introduced and spread simultaneously with Theravāda Buddhism," had "extensive structural and functional links" with it, and eventually led to the connections whereby "village practitioners of Folk Brahman specialties" began "to identify themselves as Buddhists [and] . . . not as adherents of Brāhmanism."

There are syncretical implications also in Kirsch's observation that the Buddhist cosmological scheme became shared by the Thai Folk Brahmanic polytheism and the Thai Folk Animism which have "no distinctive and coherent world-view" of their own. Moreover, the same Buddhism by which the <u>other-worldly</u> aspirations of the monastic Buddhists in Thailand were legitimated also legitimates the <u>this-worldly</u> motivations behind the merit-making "Folk Brahman rituals" of the Thai Buddhist laity. The Buddhist cosmology provides the theistic superstructure for this system and imparts a "Buddhist" ethos and character to all parts of the Thai religious totality. The different strata of the Buddhist society have appropriated and express their Buddhist heritage in different forms and different ways. The monks do not espouse <u>all</u> the forms of Buddhism practiced by the laity but they nevertheless recognize and authorize them thereby making them parts of their Buddhist tradition. The laity do not practice the monastic forms of the Buddhist tradition, yet they materially support them, emotionally idealize them, and acquire religious merit through serving them. These relations, accordingly, indicate an organic integrality which overrides the compartmentalistic distinctions which Kirsch drew through his concept of social variance and qualify in important respects his perspective on Thai Buddhism and his recapitulation (1977:263f.) of Thailand's religious history.

Chapter Five. Conclusions: The Socio-Historical Explanation of Theravāda Buddhism

This discussion of the distinctive historical perspective on Theravāda Buddhism introduced by sociologists into their interpretations of its South and Southeast Asia socio-cultural contexts has shown their progression from a structural-functional emphasis during the nineteen-sixties toward a distinctive "socio-historical" perspective before the end of the nineteen-seventies. This methodological shift moved in tandem with changing perceptions of the character of Theravāda Buddhism and of its historical evolution as the religion of South Asia's Theravāda Buddhists. These progressions also presented the topics and agenda for the comprehensive review and revision of the current academic historiography on Theravāda Buddhism in South and Southeast Asia which Manning Nash had foreseen early in the nineteen-sixties.

A. The Unfinished Agenda in the Socio-History of Theravāda Buddhism

The sociological field-data had exposed to view the wide disparities of belief and practice between the "normative" Theravāda Buddhism espoused by South Asia's Theravāda Buddhist elites and the "historic" Theravāda Buddhist "religion" practiced by the general population of its "Theravāda Buddhists." The "traditional" nature of these contrasting belief-systems demanded a scientific explanation of Theravāda Buddhism's historical and sociological dimensions. But while its historical explanation primarily depended upon the Buddhist scriptural and historiographical traditions behind the current "histories" of Theravāda Buddhism, its sociological explanation stemmed from present-day Buddhist field-data which brought to light a crucial distinction between "normative" and "historic" Theravāda

Buddhism. Moreover, although the social scientists did not assume responsibility for revising the current academic histories of Theravāda Buddhism, the historical bearings of their researches on "traditional" religions in Buddhist South Asia indicated the necessity for such revision and review for an empirically and historically valid account of Theravāda Buddhism in South Asia.

The foregoing review of their published researches, however, indicates the handicaps preventing this revolutionary sociological contribution to a socio-history of Theravāda Buddhism. For so long as the primary focus of their socio-anthropological interest remained during the nineteen-sixties upon the folk-religion and its connections with the popular religion of South Asia's Theravāda Buddhists, they could not do empirical and historical justice to the mixed Theravāda Buddhism generated by infusions of folk-religion with Theravāda Buddhist elements. Their limited anthropological perspective on the folk-religion prevented a crucial recognition of the popular religion as a facet or component of the historic South Asian Theravāda Buddhism itself. Instead, they conceptually compartmentalized in the religion of South Asia's Theravada Buddhist peasant-folk and urban-folk three, five, eight, or even eleven historically distinct traditions; then they deleted "Theravāda" and "Buddhism" labels from most of these and reserved the "Theravāda" label solely for one.

In this regard, the social scientists assumed the historical validity of the current academic history of Theravāda Buddhism and imported its presuppositions and assumptions into their interpretations and explanations of it even at a time when modern historians of Buddhism were beginning to recognize the unhistorical features of a monastically-biassed Theravāda Buddhist historiography and even at the time when a few of them - notably Heinz Bechert - were beginning to recognize the gifted leadership of socio-anthropologists opening to view the socio-cultural worlds of early, medieval and modern Buddhist South Asia and providing empirically-sound specific and general information on the "traditional" character and the history of Buddhism in South and Southeast Asia.

Their scientific contribution to the history of Buddhism stemmed, however, from their sociological interest in Theravāda Buddhism's religious complexity and its interpretation and explanation in terms of the socio-cultural conditions, forces, and processes which must have shaped its early, medieval, and modern actualizations in each of the "Theravāda Buddhist" countries of South and Southeast Asia. Their specific sociological insights on Theravāda Buddhist history appeared in regard to the diverse systems of Theravāda Buddhism and the respective social groupings in Theravāda Buddhist South Asia which had adopted and displayed them in varying degrees and dimensions. The empirical and historical validity of their sociological representations of the traditional Theravāda Buddhism in South Asia initially rested upon the theoretical validity of the concepts and hypotheses behind the socio-cultural paradigm developed by the "Chicago School" in regard to the dynamic of "Great Tradition/Little Tradition" interaction forming hybrid or "heterogenetic" cultures and religions. But the historiographical value of their interpretations could only be minimal so long as they were directed toward validating the Redfield-Marriott dichotomy while respecting the prestigious older view of Theravāda Buddhism and its history among the Buddhist textual-historians.

The methodological procedures which individual social scientists adopted also affected the historiographical viability of their findings and interpretations. The primary data-collective approach of the sociologists, through questionnaires and interviews, forced the responses into the conceptual dichotomy of the Great Tradition and the Little Tradition. In particular, Ames' and Spiro's studies show how much the answers of respondents to their questions nicely fitted their theoretical predilections. More appropriate "non-reactive techniques" of indirect inquiry could have provided scientifically more trustworthy information and relevant interpretational extrapolations covering extensive time-periods and disclosing important and hitherto unobvious differences, anomalies, inconsistencies, and historical changes. For example, S.J. Tambiah's studies of religion in Thailand exceptionally indicate the kind and range of historical extrapolations which the rule of cultural continuity and transformation indicated by Michael B. Schiffer in "Methodological Issues in Ethnoarcheology" (1978) make interpretatively viable. In essence, the rule implies that the present complexity of the traditional religion in contemporary Thailand is the latest repetition of spacial and material interrelations which also formed its complexity in the past. Hence, those complex organizations can now be "recollected" through retrospective extrapolations from it.

When Schiffer explained this historically-retrospective methodology of ethnoarcheology in the late nineteen-seventies, it was barely past its beginnings. Likewise, Tambiah's retrospectional "socio-historical" or "socio-cultural-historical" approach to the ritual expressions of Thai Buddhism was only at its beginnings. Nevertheless, he climaxed a significant period of sociological input on the history of Buddhism in South Asia showing how the concepts and theory behind the new science of sociology developed by Emile Durkheim, William James, B. Malinowski, Max Weber, and Levi-Strauss could be fruitfully applied to the cause of an empirically-sound and authentic modern "history" or "socio-history" of Theravāda Buddhism.

It is not surprising that the highly visible profile of the modern forms of the Buddhist religious tradition in South Asia attracted Tambiah's generation of social scientists who recognized the diagnostic value of contemporary political, economic and religious movements for understanding a society's social life, its present vitality or stagnation, and symptoms of "social pathology," and so on. These scientists perceived that the religious component of the Buddhist socio-culture in South and Southeast Asia is not solely a psychical phenomenon, nor its expressions merely, in Jan de Vries' words (1967:156-161), "hypostasizations of society." They are composite socio-cultural systems reflecting the diverse reciprocal interrelations of older and newer forms of Buddhism, the conditions and processes of Buddhist historical development behind the mechanisms of "buddhaization" of aboriginal systems and "indigenization" of imported Buddhist traditions, and the broader syncretizing dynamic through which Theravāda Buddhism unfolded its successive transformations from early to modern times. Even the regional socio-cultural contextualizations of temporally and spacially localized "Theravāda Buddhism" in South Asia are crucial indicators of both its "inner history" or regionally determined modifications of its ideological, ritual, and institutional structure, and of its "outer history" or fortunes along the "corridors" of its expansion from mainland India into Southeast Asia from early to modern times.

The scientists drew their distinctive historical insights from the divergent and variant mainstream and marginal, denominational and sectarian, and cultic and animistic forms of the regional Buddhism in each of the Theravāda Buddhist countries of South and Southeast Asia. Their perceptive insights regarding the present carriers of the Buddhist tradition, and the present forms in which the present and the past of the tradition are melded, made them composers of a second historiographical testimony on Theravāda Buddhism complementing, supplementing, and correcting its traditional historiographical records. Their observations provided not only the kind of explanation which Robert Ellwood (1979:71) recognized in "the best historical studies" of religions, but also the "hard quantified base" which Ellwood thought was "urgently needed in a field where writers without empirical control tend to soar off into aquarian or alarmist stratospheres."

Their published researches also indicated a fundamental historiographical point that religions are not empirically reducible solely to systems of ideas. Religions are complexes of beliefs, values, rituals and institutions of peoples living in societies. Their ancient socio-cultures have preserved and perpetuated the traditions in which those beliefs and practices have become normatively defined and authoritatively sanctioned. Furthermore, since each "traditional" religion mirrors the complexity of its matrical socio-culture, its historical and sociological explanations properly include a socio-historical retrospection working from its present formations through each of its preceding transformations back to its origins.

Since the complexity of contemporary South Asian Buddhism comprises a plurality of component-systems, its monolithic Theravāda Buddhist "component" is conceptually isolable but is not empirically separable from it. In other words, no "normative" Theravāda Buddhism can be supposed to have actually existed outside of the larger religious complexity at any time or stage of Buddhist history in South and Southeast Asia. Accordingly, the tendency among sociologists for separating "normative Theravāda Buddhism" from "the religion of South Asia's Theravāda Buddhists" and removing it from the arena of their sociological inquiries could not be scientifically justified. The tendency had to be reversed once the "component" character of Theravāda Buddhism became recognized. This realization is apparently behind the interpretational "shifts" in their earlier and later published researches from a "monolithic" to a "polylithic" or pluralistic view and definition of the historic Theravāda Buddhism which had been so largely overlooked by academic historians of Buddhism.

This "shift," however, was only a "trend." It did not lead to any general consensus and decision on the sociological study of Theravāda Buddhism in South and Southeast Asia. In the later work of S.J. Tambiah, the "trend" appears in the shape of an wholistic and organic view of Theravāda Buddhism encompassing the kaleidoscope of dynamically interrelated stratified levels through which it became historically articulated within the socio-culture and religion of South and Southeast Asia's Theravāda Buddhist populations. The culmination of this "trend," moreover, would be the fulfilment of the socio-anthropological mandate on Theravāda Buddhism which Manning Nash had envisaged in the early nineteen-sixties as entailing a comprehensive review and revision of the

current historiography of Theravāda Buddhism in South
and Southeast Asia.

B. The Kuhnian Revolution in the Sociology of Buddhism

Despite the revolutionizing historiographical
implications of the sociological researches on religions
in Buddhist South Asia, the response by academic
historians toward the review and revision of the current
"history" of Buddhism has been tardy and piecemeal. One
reason could be the transitory functionality of the
Redfield-Marriott dichotomy itself particularly on
account of misapplications of the "Great Tradition" and
"Little Tradition" concepts to Buddhism and its
relations in South Asia. Doubts doubts about the
interpretive applicability of the Redfield-Marriott
dichotomy to Buddhism in South Asia were expressed even
by sociologists who used it extensively in modified
versions for their interpretations of contemporary South
Asian Theravāda Buddhism.

When these applicational modifications are arranged
in a temporal sequence, they appear to illustrate the
Kuhnian phenomena of "paradigm-shift" leading to
"paradigm-change" and the "crisis" of the
incompatibility of the dual Great Tradition/Little
Tradition Theravāda Buddhism of South Asia's Theravāda
Buddhists and the Great Tradition of normative Theravāda
Buddhism drawn from the canonical scriptures by the
Theravāda Buddhist monastic order. In other words,
awareness of the incongruity between the Theravāda
Buddhist "Great Tradition" and the kaleidoscopic
religious "Little Tradition" of South Asia's Theravāda
Buddhist population gradually eroded the
interpretational functionality of Redfield's paradigm
and paved the way for alternative paradigms.
Nevertheless, although this "paradigm shift" and change
was on a less dramatic scale than the paradigm shifts

and changes illustratively used by Thomas S. Kuhn in The
Structure of Scientific Revolutions (1970), the
modifications made to the concepts and theory behind
Redfield's paradigm of peasant socio-cultures in order
to interrelate the normative and non-normative forms and
expressions of the religion of South Asia's Theravāda
Buddhists reflect a pattern of sociological paradigm
change having important bearings upon the scientific
study of, and historical knowledge about, South Asian
Buddhism.

Even the tidal "shift" from the purely "academic"
historical study of Theravāda Buddhism to its "socio-
historical" study fits Kuhn's characterization of a
"scientific revolution." Redfield's concepts and theory
of "Great Tradition" and "Little Tradition" and their
interactions and the data of folk-religions in Buddhist
South Asia provided interpretive "nuclei of an
unprecedented scientific achievement" - using Kuhn's
words - by "an enduring group of adherents" drawn away
from other and "competing modes of scientific inquiry"
and seeking true and relevant resolutions of "all sorts
of problems" concerning the character and history of
Theravāda Buddhism in the socio-cultural context of
South Asia's peasant-folk Theravāda Buddhists.
Unprecedented applications to religions of the concepts
of "Great Tradition" and "Little Tradition" by Redfield,
Marriott, Singer, and other associates in the Chicago
School of Anthropology launched the new phase of modern
socio-anthropological research on Hinduism and Buddhism
in South Asia. The paradigm indicated new explorational
paths and methods, new problems of scientific interest,
and new interpretational and explanational resolutions
of scientific problems represented by the religious
complexity in Buddhist South Asia.

The new phase of socio-anthropological research on the religions had its beginnings in the cognitive first-stage of "information-gathering" in the field of Buddhist South Asian religions during the early nineteen-sixties. It then proceeded into the higher cognitive levels of systems-analysis and functional analysis employed by the so-called "structural-functionalists" during the later nineteen-sixties. It finally culminated in the more intuitive esoteric concerns of scientific "meaning" and "explanation" of those religions out of which emerged the "socio-historical approach" envisaged by Tambiah toward the end of the nineteen-seventies. In all respects, Redfield's socio-anthropological paradigm met Kuhn's scientific model (1970:18-22) in regard to its presuppositional "more rigid definition of its field of inquiry" and of the problems proper to its scientific investigation. Obeyesekere typically followed other socio-anthropologists by indicating the field of his socio-anthropological investigation of religions in South Asia as being the peasant socio-culture and its pervasion by the "Great Tradition" of Theravāda Buddhism. The paradigm also indicated lines of scientific inquiry into the religious dimensions of the urban socio-cultures in Buddhist South Asia and their "Great Tradition/Little Tradition" structural and functional interrelations. By approaching these inquiries through the theory and methodology behind Redfield's paradigm of peasant socio-cultures, Obeyesekere led the way for a new scientific community whose members adopted its theoretical and methodological presuppositions and approach to South Asian religions, jointly raised and debated the issues which its interpretational applications generated, and worked toward a scientific consensus on the "real" history of Theravāda Buddhism in South and Southeast Asia.

Even the "lack of consensus" behind the debate reflected in the criticisms of each other's assumptions and the pitfalls which were mutually indicated in their researches constitute the dialectic of a distinct scientific community as defined by Kuhn (1970:52f.), joining together scientists engaged in the same scientific enterprise, sharing a common scientific- i.e. "socio-anthropological" - perspective, coming from similar professional backgrounds and training, pursuing common goals related to the same "field" of scientific inquiry, and contributing individually to the "steady extension of the scope and precision of [their] scientific knowledge" in the "highly cumulative enterprise" of the modern historical understanding of Theravāda Buddhism in contemporary South and Southeast Asia.

Kuhn indicated that one crucial test of any new line of inquiry is the "new and unsuspected phenomena" encountered within the extended boundaries of scientific knowledge which the paradigm has opened. The test for the paradigm is its interpretive capacity for normalizing or making anticipative the new data within its theoretical or interpretive framework. A cumulation of impervious new data could lead toward a breakdown of confidence in the interpretive viability of the paradigm, that is, to "paradigm crisis." The "breakdown" becomes apparent when the adaptability of the paradigm to the novel scientific data is no longer evident. The adaptability of Redfield's socio-cultural paradigm toward novel features in the religion of the Theravāda Buddhist peasant-folk in South Asia "proved" the paradigm, that is, justified its theoretical framework. On the other hand, successive adaptational

modifications of the paradigm to fit unanticipated
features of the Buddhist folk-religion show the
direction of the scientific inquiry taken by the two
distinguishable groups identified by Kirsch (1977)
respectively as the group of scientists adopting a
"structural-functional approach" to their scientific
data on South Asian religions, and the group of
scientists adopting an "historical" or "socio-historical
approach" to their field-data.

Each of these groups encountered Kuhnian "novelties
of fact" in the religion of South Asia's Theravāda
Buddhists which could not be fully explained within the
current conceptual and theoretical framework of the
Redfieldian paradigm, principally in respect of its
theoretical dynamics of "Great Tradition" and "Little
Tradition" interaction. In the South Asian religion-
field of their inquiries, the most striking anomalies
and novelties appear to have been animistic and
supernaturalistic elements and features of the popular
religion of South Asia's Theravāda Buddhist populations
precluded from the normative definition of the Theravāda
Buddhist "Great Tradition." The disparity between the
"real" or "historic" Theravāda Buddhism of the Buddhist
majority and the "ideal" Theravāda Buddhism of the
Theravāda Buddhist minority could be explained through
the "Great Tradition/Little Tradition" dichotomy itself.
But this explanation demanded a revised conception of
Theravāda Buddhism or else a modification of its "Great
Tradition" characterization to admit the reality of both
its "great tradition" and "little tradition" dimensions.
Instead, the social scientists usually modified the
paradigm to accommodate and assimilate each and every
novelty in "the religion" of the Theravāda Buddhist
majority, but not the normative "Great Tradition" of
Theravāda Buddhism.

This exclusion, on the other hand, could not be sustained indefinitely. This is because the various discovered "anomalies" in the religion of South Asia's Theravāda Buddhist population could not be "normalized" or transformed into "predicted and expected" characteristics of their "Theravāda Buddhist religion" without a substantive redefinition of Theravāda Buddhism itself and of its historic relation to the "little tradition" in South Asia's Theravāda Buddhist religion. In this regard, therefore, a breaking-point appeared inevitable in the interpretive uses of Redfield's paradigm beyond which it could no longer be sustained. The recognition of this eventual non-viability constituted the Kuhnian "paradigm crisis" in the late nineteen-seventies prior to a "paradigm replacement" or "paradigm change" in the sociological study of Buddhism in South Asia.

During the period of the nineteen-sixties and seventies, the "crisis" mounted through the cumulus of modificational shifts and changes in the concepts and theory in the paradigm culminating in a loss of faith in its viability as an explanational tool for Buddhism. The earlier endorsement of the paradigm among scientists adopting "the structural-functional approach" during the nineteen-sixties gradually shifted through mounting criticism of the paradigm and its implicit assumptions during the nineteen-seventies among scientists developing the "socio-historical approach." Before the end of the nineteen-seventies, Tambiah had climaxed the earlier critique by Dumont and Pocock by its virtual replacement by an organically schematized pluralistic paradigm of Buddhist socio-cultures. The scientific study of Theravāda Buddhism between the nineteen-fifties and the nineteen-eighties, accordingly, was a Kuhnian "scientific revolution" which may have eclipsed yet

never superceded the textual-historical paradigm behind
the older, more prestigious academic historiography of
Theravāda Buddhism.

In this context, the words "revolution,"
"revolutionary," and "revolutionizing" have specific
academic meanings. In the history of science,
"revolutions" comprise - according to Bernard Cohen
(1984) and his reviewer David Papineau (1985) - "giant
steps forward that give us altogether a new perspective
on the natural world." The sociological explorations of
religions in Buddhist South Asia, provided this kind of
revolutionizing scientific perspective on the character
and history of Theravāda Buddhism in South Asia. The
perspective was "new" or "revolutionary" in the Kuhnian
sense of being "evidentially incommensurable with the
old" academic-historical perspective, but not in the
sense of a total rejection of the older perspective. It
was not "revolutionary" on account of being recognized
as "revolutionary" by the pioneers of its distinctive
applications to Theravāda Buddhism in South Asia. It
was "new" and "revolutionary" in Papineau's sense that
it proceeded from a "transforming" set of new concepts
and theoretical assumptions which had been recently
developed in the Chicago School and illustratively
applied with promising results to the religions of
Indian South Asia. Yet since it did not replace the
current older academic-historical perspective, it may be
regarded as "complementary" to it in the Popperian sense
that revolutionary scientific ideas correct the errors
and imprecisions of earlier scientific ideas, and in the
Kuhnian sense - noted by Papineau - that new ideas
sometimes "involve wholesale conceptual reorganizations
in which all previous assumptions [come] . . . to be
seen in a new light."

It is in this "light," accordingly, that the two decades of socio-anthropological researches on religions in Buddhist South Asia can be historically estimated. For twenty years some twenty or more scholars had been professionally devoted to the pursuit of a new scientific understanding of the religion espoused by the large majority of South Asia's Theravāda Buddhists. During the two decades, scholars researching in the same "field" of empirical inquiry applied Robert Redfield's socio-cultural paradigm to their data, built upon the scientific observations and religion-interpretive conclusions of their colleagues, and worked toward a consensus on Theravāda Buddhism relating its "real" character and "history" to the historiography of "normative Theravāda Buddhism" studied by Buddhist-textual historians. Yet only in retrospect, when their work was finally completed, because the paradigm which informed it had become superceded by a different system of socio-cultural concepts and theories, could their individual contributions to the scientific understanding of Theravāda Buddhism be garnered into a summational socio-anthropological statement concerning the real character and history of Theravāda Buddhism in South Asia. This summation in turn has become the new historical testimony on Theravāda Buddhism in South Asia. It is no longer possible for historians of religions to write competently about any phase of Theravāda Buddhist history without drawing upon the substantive empirical and historical conclusions about Theravāda Buddhism which the social scientists unfolded.

C. Theravāda Buddhism in its Sociological Representations

The sociological studies of Buddhism in South Asia show the variety of symbolical, metaphorical, allegorical and suchlike configurations which they and

their contemporaries in other disciplines used for
imaginatively representing the complexity of Theravāda
Buddhism in its socio-cultural contexts. These figures
reflect their conceptual, theoretical and methodological
stances, and their individual understandings of the
componential complexity of the religious system which
has been espoused by South Asia's Theravāda Buddhists in
the past as well as in the present. The diversity of
the configurations, on the other hand, indicates the
besetting problems behind the lack of consensus on the
character and development of Theravāda Buddhism in South
Asia. Nevertheless, their sequential arrangement into
earlier and later representations could display
interpretational transitions in their scientific
understanding of the religions of Buddhist South Asia
throughout the nineteen-sixties and seventies in the
light of the structural-functionalistic approach which
predominated throughout the nineteen-sixties and of the
socio-historical approach which became prominent during
the nineteen-seventies.

The interpretive utility of these configurations
stems in part from the economical precision of their
systemic representation of the parts and components of
the complex religious metasystems in Buddhist South
Asia. On the other hand, their interpretational
viability depended essentially upon the theoretical
presuppositions and the methodological approaches which
shaped them. There are noticeable differences, for
example, between the architectonic configurations
displaying the theoretical and methodological
orientations of the earlier structural-functionalistic
sociological approaches to the religions, and the
organic configurations displaying the socio-historical
or cultural-historical sociological approaches of the
seventies. The contrast between the static

architectonic configurational imagery of the early
structuralistic representations and the dynamic organic
metaphors of the later socio-historical representations
may be merely formal and due to whether or not only one
or several or all of the essential components and
features of the religious complexes are intended to be
represented, although it does seem that scientists used
the more dynamic organic configurations for representing
the complexity wherever a socio-historical approach was
adopted.

The more "organic" traditional and modern
imaginative configurations and representations, such as
the classical early Buddhist allegory of the Wish-
fulfilling Tree, could display all the relational
variables of a religion, and anticipate variations
consequent upon changes in its socio-cultural
environment whereas the architectonic representational
schema could not do so. Tambiah criticized Michael
Ames' architectonic representation of the total
religious system of the Sinhalese as being rigid and a-
historical. Other imaginative configurations employing
the architectural and archeological metaphors of
"strata" and "levels," and the fixed geometrical
configurations of the circle, the pyramid, or the square
could hardly represent the dynamic structural and
functional interrelations comprising the complexity of
the pluralistic religion of South Asia's Theravāda
Buddhists.

Obeyesekere's imaginative representation of
Theravāda Buddhism as the overarching normative scheme
of reference for the down-to-earth Buddhism of the
masses indicates an unreal spacial and ideological
"distancing" between the Buddhism of the general public
and the Buddhism of South Asia's Buddhist elites of
monks, scholars, and intellectuals. Linear

configurations using the metaphors of the river or the railway track found in recent imaginative representations of Buddhism in South Asia are likewise problematic. Melford E. Spiro's description of Burmese Buddhism implies a single-line-track image of Theravāda Buddhism winding an independent course across the vast terrain of South and Southeast Asian socio-cultures and remaining uncontaminated by any contacts with the aboriginal religion of Burma's masses. A double-track metaphor in Trevor Ling's account of The Buddha: Buddhist Civilization in India and Ceylon (1973) indicates the distinct and independent courses of Buddhism and folk-religion in the history of Sinhalese religion, although he doubted that the folk-stream could be set alongside Buddhism under the category of "religion."

The more dynamic linear imagery in Robert Redfield's explanation of the interaction of "Great Tradition" and "Little Tradition" religion in terms of "two streams continuously flowing into and out of each other" precluded that interflow from becoming an historic mergence of the two religious "streams" in Buddhist South Asia. Philip Ashby's conceptual delineation of Buddhism in History and Future of Religious Thought: Christianity, Hinduism, Buddhism, Islam (1963) depicts its logical progression: "beginning as a way of release, it flowered into a code of earthly conduct, a method of intellectual endeavour, a system of metaphysical speculation and belief, and a way of religious worship." Such an abstracted view of Buddhism's historical development demands a socio-cultural background. Ashby appears to have been aware of this deficiency in his prophetic anticipation of a "new religious thinking" among historians and social scientists about Buddhism's "cultural ethos" as being

"not limited to a specific culture or form of society,"
but adaptively integrated with "indigenous traditions"
along the course of "its cultural and geographical
expansion" whereby local traditions became "forced to
bring themselves in line with the essentials which
constitute the historic character of Buddhism" while
Buddhism was forced also into "the dilution of [its]
initial insights."

Ashby anticipated a new scientific understanding
of Buddhism in: its historic "dialectical relationship
with other religions and cultures"; its inherently
dynamic flexible self-adjustment "within the advanced
cultures" of Northeast Asia; and the historical outcome
of a Buddhist plurality comprising a functional
association of Buddhist "local cults and national
religions" emerging as "less an international religion
and more a collection of local religions each somewhat
distinct from one another." The imagery indicated by
his socio-historical mandate could be a temporal flow
chart surmounted on a spacial "histomap" showing the
peaks and troughs of Buddhism's temporal growth and
spacial expansion in mainland India and further Indian
South Asia.

A linear sequential arrangement of the sociological
representations of Buddhism would show the
interpretational "shift" from the greater separation of
the Theravāda Buddhist "Great Tradition" from the
"Little Tradition" religion of South Asia's Theravāda
Buddhists to the greater integration of the two
traditions. The earlier emphasis upon the separation of
the two traditions is apparent in Obeyesekere's
representation of the Sinhalese religion in the socio-
cultural context of the "Theravāda Buddhist countries"
of South Asia. It shows the normative Theravāda
Buddhism as the source of ideal values for the Sinhalese

religion. But it does not clearly indicate whether or not the Sinhalese religion and its neighbouring counterparts are interpretable aboriginal religions or regionally-formulated versions of a pan-South-Asian Theravāda Buddhism, or are "non-Buddhist religions" sharing acquired Buddhist elements, features, influences, or having a functional complementarity with Buddhism, and even receiving a "tolerated" Buddhist authorization. The interpretational option that Obeyesekere preferred may be indicated by the three basic propositions underlying his imaginative representation of religions in Buddhist South Asia.

SINHALESE BUDDHISM (GANGANATH OBEYESEKERE'S MODEL, 1963)

OBEYESEKERE'S HYPOTHESES

1. SINHALESE RELIGION CANNOT BE EQUATED WITH THERAVĀDA BUDDHISM.

2. SINHALESE RELIGION COMPRISES AN INTEGRATED TRADITION OF THERAVĀDA AND NON-THERAVĀDA RELIGIOUS BELIEFS AND PRACTICES.

3. SINHALESE BUDDHISM IS A DISTINCTIVE RELIGIOUS TRADITION HAVING:
    VARIOUS LEVELS OF BELIEFS,
    AN INFRASTRUCTURAL UNIFICATION OF THOSE "LEVELS", AND
    A SYMBIOTIC AND DIALECTICAL IDEOLOGICAL RELATION WITH THE "GREAT TRADITION" OF THERAVĀDA BUDDHISM.

SINHALESE RELIGION (MICHAEL AMES' MODEL, 1964)

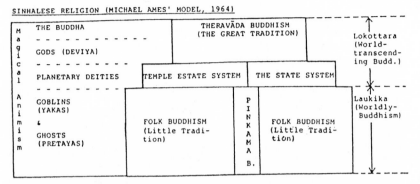

AMES' PROPOSITIONS

1. SINHALESE RELIGION SHOWS A PYRAMIDICAL TWO-TIER STRUCTURE. FOLK-BUDDHISM IS ITS BASE AND COMPRISES THE RELIGION OF THE PEASANT MASSES. THE GREAT TRADITION OF THERAVADA BUDDHISM IS THE RELIGION OF THE ELITES AND REPRESENTS THE SINHALESE RELIGIOUS APEX.

2. MERIT-MAKING (PINKAMA) BUDDHISM IS THE POPULAR CORE LINKING THE LITTLE TRADITION FOLK-BUDDHISM WITH THE GREAT TRADITION THERAVADA BUDDHISM.

3. THE "NON-BUDDHIST" "ESTATE" AND "STATE" SYSTEMS PROVIDE ECONOMIC AND POLITICAL SUPPORTS FOR THE INSTITUTIONAL GREAT TRADITION BUDDHISM.

4. MAGICAL-ANIMISM IS A "NON-RELIGIOUS" COMPLEMENTATION OF THE THERAVADA AND THE FOLK BUDDHISMS AND IS INTEGRAL TO NEITHER SYSTEMS.

Michael Ames' conceptual representation of the "total religious system of the Sinhalese" has a pyramidical form, having Magical-animism as a supporting buttress for the four social strata of the monks, the monarchy, the urban middle-class and the peasant folk. His sociological representation emphasizes the religion's structural and functional dichotomies of "great tradition" and "little tradition," "Buddhism" and "non-Buddhism," "other-worldly" and "this-worldly" orientations, "religion" and "magic," and "propitiatory animism" and "merit-making popular Buddhism." Ames' imaginative configuration manifestly contrasts with Hans-Dieter Evers' representation in which he equated Sinhalese religion with "Theravada Buddhism" but recognized in it three contradictory systemic expressions.

SINHALESE RELIGION (HANS-DEITER EVERS' MODEL, 1972)

```
                 ┌─── SINHALESE RELIGION = THERAVĀDA BUDDHISM ───┐
                 │              (Three component subsystems)      │
  VIHARE BUDDHISM ─ ─ ─ ─ DEVALE BUDDHISM ─ ─ ─ ─ ROYAL BUDDHISM
```

EVERS' PROPOSITIONS

1. SINHALESE RELIGION IS A REGIONAL TYPE OF THERAVĀDA BUDDHISM.

2. THIS SINHALESE BUDDHISM COMPRISES THREE CONTRASTING CONTEMPORANEOUS SUB-
   SYSTEMS.

3. EACH SUBSYSTEM IS A DISTINCTIVE BUDDHIST COMPLEX COMPRISING SUPERNATURAL
   POWERS (REFERENTS), RELIGIOUS SPECIALISTS, DISTINCTIVE RITUALS, AND
   DISTINCTIVE SOCIAL AND ECONOMIC ORGANIZATIONS.

Heinz Bechert's imaginative representation of Ceylon's Buddhistic religion reflects a maturation of the structural-functionalist approach to South Asia's religions. Its uniqueness, however, is his attachment of the "Great Tradition/Little Tradition" dichotomy both to the popular religion of the Sinhalese and their elite Buddhist religion, and his singular portrayal of the polylithic character of the Theravāda buddhaized religion of Ceylon's Buddhists. Another distinctive feature is his recognition of a national cultus interconnecting Sinhalese aboriginal and indigenous religions with Buddhism.

SINHALESE RELIGION (HEINZ BECHERT'S MODEL, 1978)

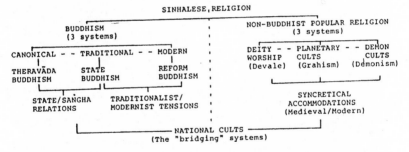

BECHERT'S PROPOSITIONS

1. MODERN SINHALESE RELIGION IS A COMPLEXITY WHICH COMPRISES FOUR COMPONENT RELIGIONS.
2. THESE COMPONENTS COMPRISE THE RELIGIOUS COMPLEXITY IN ALL THERAVĀDA BUDDHIST COUNTRIES, NAMELY: NORMATIVE (THERAVĀDA) BUDDHISM, POPULAR BUDDHISM, HALF-MAGICAL PRACTICES, AND NON-BUDDHIST CULTS.
3. BUDDHISM HOWEVER, HAS NEVER EXISTED AS A "PURELY RELIGIOUS THEORY" BUT ALWAYS AS THIS INTEGRATED SYNCRETIC SYSTEM.
4. NATIONAL CULTS PROVIDE THE BRIDGING CONNECTION BETWEEN RURAL-VILLAGE DEMON-CULTS AND BUDDHISM.
5. NEVERTHELESS, THESE COMPONENTIAL DISTINCTIONS DO NOT EMPIRICALLY EXIST AS HISTORICALLY DISTINCT SYSTEMS BUT ARE COGNIZABLE PLANES WHICH CANNOT BE SHARPLY DIFFERENTIATED FROM EACH OTHER.

The clear-cut dichotomies drawn by social scientists into the Sinhalese religion are less emphasized in studies of <u>Burmese</u> religion which show Theravāda Buddhism as more or less submerged in the aboriginal pre-Buddhist supernaturalism. In Brohm's imaginative representation of the Burmese religion, he seems to have resurrected late nineteenth- and early twentieth-century versions of the "thin veneer" theory of Burmese religion in regard to the survival of a pre-Buddhist animism under the cover of Theravāda Buddhism. In Burma, accordingly, traditional Theravāda Buddhism has the character of a buddhaized Burmese-animism.

BURMESE RELIGION (JOHN BROHM'S MODEL, 1963)

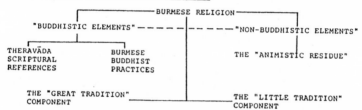

BROHM'S PROPOSITIONS

1. BURMESE RELIGION IS A REGIONAL MODE OF THERAVĀDA BUDDHISM WHICH COMPRISES INTEGRATED "BUDDHIST" AND "ANIMISTIC" COMPONENTS.

2. THIS SYNCRETIC COMPLEX IS PERCEIVED AS "THERAVĀDA BUDDHISM" BY THE BURMESE "WHO CERTAINLY REGARD THEMSELVES AS THERAVĀDA BUDDHISTS."

3. "ALL OBJECTIVE REPORTS SPEAK IN GREATER OR LESSER DETAIL OF RESIDUAL ELEMENTS IN BUDDHISM WHICH OWE LITTLE OR NOTHING TO BUDDHISM." THE REPORTS REFER TO THESE AS "ANIMISM" AND "POSIT THESE ANIMISTIC ELEMENTS AS RELIGIOUS ALTERNATIVES TO BUDDHISM."

4. BUDDHISM AS <u>PRACTICED</u> IN BURMA IS A FORM OF ANIMISM. ANIMISM IS THE MORE ANCIENT, LESS ORGANIZED FAITH. BUDDHISM IS THE MORE RECENT, PHILOSOPHICALLY ORIENTED AND CANONICAL FAITH.

5. THE "SCRIPTURAL REFERENTS" OF THE BURMESE RELIGION ARE "THERAVĀDA BUDDHISM" YET "ITS PRACTICAL CHARACTERISTICS TEND TO BE TRADITIONAL BUT ARE NOT NECESSARILY SCRIPTURALLY DERIVED.

6. MEMBERS OF THE SOCIAL ELITE APPEAR TO POSSESS A LARGER SHARE OF THE "GREAT TRADITION" WHILE THE MASSES "FILL THEIR RELIGIOUS WORLD WITH PEASANT SUPERSTITIONS."

7. THE RELIGION OF "THE MAJORITY OF BURMESE" IS ACCORDINGLY AN ADMIXTURE OF ANIMISTIC, SUPERNATURALISTIC AND BUDDHIST RELIGIONS.

Melford E. Spiro's imaginative representation of the Burmese religion (1967,1970) reflects his strong anthropological interest in "the Nat-cultures" and its enlivening influence upon Theravāda Buddhism in Burma, and his sense of the strong dualities found in Ames' Sinhalese-religion studies, yet qualified by Brohm's insistence upon the integral unity of Burma's syncretic Theravāda Buddhist religion and its counterparts in the rest of regional Buddhist South Asia.

BURMESE RELIGION (MELFORD E. SPIRO'S MODEL, 1967, 1970)

```
                          BURMESE RELIGION
         ┌──────────────────────┴──────────────────────────┐
"THE NAT CULTUS" - - - - - - - - - - - - - - - - - - THERAVĀDA BUDDHISM
                  (influence and enliven)                  │
                                        THERAVĀDA BUDDHIST SYSTEMS
   ┌───────────────────┬─────────────────────┬─────────────┐
"NIBBANIC"          "KAMMATIC"           "APOTROPAIC"   "ESOTERIC"
BUDDHISM            BUDDHISM             BUDDHISM       BUDDHISM
                                                       (2 systems)
                                            ┌──────────────┴────────┐
                                        ESCHATALOGICAL      MILLENIAL
                                        BUDDHISM            BUDDHISM
                                        (Future Buddha)     (Future
                                                            King)
```

SPIRO'S PROPOSITIONS

1. "BUDDHISM" AND "THE NAT CULTUS" ARE HISTORICALLY DISTINCT RELIGIOUS
        SYSTEMS.
2. THE DISTINCTION IS EVIDENT IN THEIR CLEAR "DIVISION OF LABOR" AND
        THEIR "WORLDLY" (laukika) AND "OTHER-WORLDLY" OR "SUPERNATURAL"
        (lokuttara) JURISDICTIONS.
3. BUDDHISM HAS A PRIMACY OVER THE NAT CULTUS YET HAS AN "INSTRUMENTAL
        AFFINITY" WITH THE LATTER ON ACCOUNT OF BEING "SUBVERTED" TO
        MUNDANE PURPOSES.
4. CONTRARY TO BURMESE CLAIMS, BURMESE BUDDHISM IS NOT PURE THERAVĀDA
        BUDDHISM. NEVERTHELESS, THAT BUDDHISM - "AT LEAST IN ITS GREAT
        TRADITION ASPECTS" IS THE "TRUE RELIGION" OF THE BURMESE.
5. ITS PRIMACY FOR THE BURMESE IS EVIDENCED BY: THEIR GREATER INTEREST IN IT;
        ITS UTILITY AS THE SOURCE OF THEIR NORMATIVE IDEALS AND VALUES; ITS
        SUPERIOR POWER OVER THE "NATS"; AND ITS PSYCHOLOGICAL RELEVANCE IN
        PROJECTING THEIR "IDEAL IMPULSES ."
6. THE "NAT CULTUS" EXISTS, NOT "IN DEFIANCE" OF BUDDHISM BUT AS A PRAGMATICAL
        COMPLEMENTATION OF IT.

S.J. Tambiah's hypothetical schematization of the ritual-system in the Thai religion (1970:338) is illustratively applicable also to the total religious system of Thailand's Theravāda Buddhists.

The religious field

2 'SUKHWAN' RITUAL Household/kin/neighbours Rites of passage/threshold rites Pacha/mau khwan Theravada

1 BUDDHIST RITES Total community Collective merit-making festivals Monk Buddha household, kin and neighbours mortuary rites

household, kin and neighbours
house blessing

Bun (merit) 3 1

E D C B Khwan A Winjan
(life) (death)

4 2

Baab (demerit)

Tiam (medium)/cham (intermediary) Collective agricultural rites Guardian spirits Total community

3 CULT OF GUARDIAN SPIRITS

Malevolent spirits Mau bham (exorcist) Exorcism Patient/household Mausong (diviner) Rites of affliction

4 RITES OF MALEVOLENT SPIRITS

THAI RELIGION (TAMBIAH'S OVERVIEW, 1967, 1970)

1. THAI RELIGION IS A COMPLEX OF DIVERSE RELIGIOUS FIELDS.
2. EACH RELIGIOUS "FIELD" COMPRISES A NETWORK OF COGNIZABLY INTERRELATED STRUCTURAL COMPLEXES.
3. THE FOUR MOST DISTINCTIVE "FIELDS" AND COMPLEXES ARE: BUDDHISM, BRĀHMANISM, THE CULTS OF "GUARDIAN SPIRITS," AND THE CULTS OF MALEVOLENT SPIRITS.
4. THESE ARE COMPLEMENTARY SYSTEMIC APPROACHES TO "THE SUPERNATURAL."
5. THIS COMPLEMENTARITY, HOWEVER, DOES NOT CONFUSE THEIR IDENTITIES WITHIN THAILAND'S RELIGIOUSLY PLURALISTIC SOCIO-CULTURE.

A. Thomas Kirsch's 1977 representation of the religion of Thailand's Theravāda Buddhist reflects awareness of its polylithic complexity. His exposition of the functional interrelations of the Buddhist, Brahmanic, and Animistic subsystems mitigated the compartmentalistic extremity of earlier structuralist representations. However, he did not draw any conclusion on whether or not the Thai religion is a regional form of Theravāda Buddhism having its pre-Buddhist traditions as complementatively functioning "sectors."

THAI RELIGION (A. THOMAS KIRSCH'S MODEL, 1977)

	THAI RELIGION (3 components)		
	BUDDHISM ——	"BRĀHMANISM" ——	ANIMISM
GOAL ORIENTATION	Other-worldly	This-worldly	This-worldly
WORLD VIEW	Determinate/ Certain	Determinate/ Certain	Capricious/ Uncertain
RITUAL	Standard/ Routine	Standard/ Routine	Client Tai-lored
RITUAL SPECIALISTS	Predominantly Male	Predominantly Male	Predominantly Female
RECRUITMENT	Universalistic Achievement	Universalistic Achievement	Particularis-tic Ascrip-tion
PARTICIPANTS	Laity	Clients	Clients
INVOLVEMENT	Constant	Intermittent	Intermittent
ATTITUDE TO NATURE	Highly Favour-able	Favourable	Ambivalent
SOCIAL FOCUS	Whole society	Bridging Loca-lity and Society	Highly local-ized

KIRSCH'S PROPOSITIONS (strongly based on Ames' work)

1. THE PRINCIPAL DISTINGUISHABLE COMPONENTS OF THE THAI RELIGION ARE: THERA-VĀDA BUDDHISM, A BRAHMANISTIC ELEMENT, AND AN ANIMISTIC COMPONENT.

2. THESE ARE CONTRASTIVELY IDENTIFIABLE IN TERMS OF: GOAL ORIENTATION, WORLD VIEW, SOCIAL FOCUS, AND SPECIALISTS. HOWEVER, THEY SHARE SEVERAL FEATURES.

3. BUDDHISM IS AT THE APEX OF THE THAI RELIGIOUS SYSTEM AND IS THE CENTRAL LOCUS OF THAI SOCIAL AND ETHICAL VALUES. BRĀHMANISM AND ANIMISM ARE RELATED TO IT AS "SUBSYSTEMS."

4. THE BRAHMANIC SUBSYSTEM IS LINKED WITH THE BUDDHIST INSTITUTIONS. THE FOLK-BRĀHMANISM PROVIDES A THERAPEUTIC FUNCTION, LEGITIMATES LAY-BUDDHIST THIS-WORLDLY INVOLVEMENTS, AND IS THE NECESSARY PRACTICAL SECTOR OF THE FORMAL BUDDHISM.

5. THE THREE COMPONENTS DO NOT COMPRISE "A NEATLY INTEGRATED AND BALANCED HOMEO-STATIC SYSTEM" BUT "TENSIONS" WITHIN THE THAI RELIGIOUS COMPLEXITY .

The ideal visual representation of the Theravāda
Buddhist religion in South Asia would be a flow chart
showing the historic course of Theravāda Buddhist
development from the matrix of brahmanical, animistic,
and folk-religion in ancient India and subsequent
syncretic forms following its acculturation with
regional and local, indigenous and aboriginal, cultic
and animistic, and vaiṣṇava and mahāyāna religion
elements in South and Southeast Asia. The completion
of the flow chart "cycle" would include the manifold
syncretic expressions of the Theravāda Buddhist metasystem of "further India" and the modernizing and
westernizing conditions and forces which recently
produced the forms of it that were re-exported to India
- such as "neo-Buddhism," for example - and to further
Asia, Western Europe, and North America.

In the following biospherical flow chart on the
organic evolution of Theravāda Buddhism within and
beyond mainland India, the lithosphere represents the
"greater India" socio-cultural "region" of its
acculturation, the hydrosphere the spacial regions of
the "Theravāda Buddhist countries" in South and
Southeast Asia where it merged with pre-Buddhist
aboriginal religions and earlier Brahmanic and Mahāyāna
traditions, and the stratosphere indicates the emergent
heterogenetic Theravāda Buddhist metasystem prior to any
recent Westernizing and politicizing conditions and
influences which produced its modern transformations.

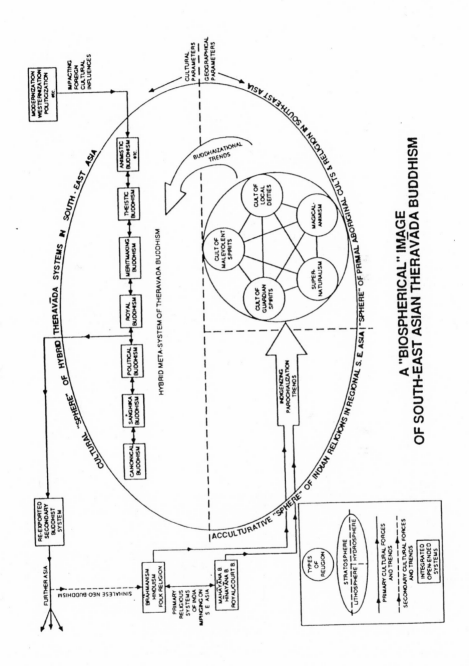

A "BIOSPHERICAL" IMAGE
OF SOUTH-EAST ASIAN THERAVĀDA BUDDHISM

Notes

Chapter One. Great Tradition and Little Tradition in the
    Sociology of Religions

[1]Robert Redfield (1955.41) noted that the conceptual distinction between the "Great Tradition" and the "Little Tradition" had been "long present in discussions of civilizations". But he also equated the concepts with "high culture" and "low culture," "learned" and "popular" traditions, and "hierarchic" and "lay" systems.

[2]Since all the known historic civilizations—including the Brahmanical and the Buddhist civilizations in ancient India - reflect the "secondary phase" of acculturational hybridization, the "orthogenetic" and "heterogenetic" conceptual distinctions may be inapplicable to them. Nevertheless, the historic outcome of orthogenetic and heterogenetic change is recognizable in the light of developmental processes which their present complexity reflects.

[3]Redfield (1955:51) supported this contention by comparisons between Vedic or Upanishadic philosophy and Hindu sectarian religion and between Taoist philosophy and religious Taoism. Yet, he might more appropriately have distinguished the professional and the nonprofessional or lay forms or "levels" of the traditions in India and China.

[4]Anthropologists interested in religions of Southeast Asia could recognize the organization of Theravāda Buddhist monasticism in urban and rural Buddhist Asia as a significant historic example of the relational complexity which Redfield indicated.

[5]McKim Marriott presented his explanation of the relationship in an essay on "Little Communities in an Indigenous Civilization" (1955) read at a seminar in social anthropology in the University of Chicago during the Spring of 1954.

[6]The issue behind this part of Marriott's discussion (1955:171-3) of the Indian village culture is whether or not a village is a socio-cultural whole or should be perceived as an elemental part or unity of the larger and more complex "great culture and society" in which it is "imbedded." Marriott's answer qualified the conceptualizations of village communities as homogenous totalities presented by Srinivas (1951:1051-1055), Miller (1952:160 & 163), Gough (1952:534), and Bailey (1953:327-328) but specifically addressed the essay by

Redfield and Milton Singer on "Comparisons of Cultures:
The Indian Village" (1954) in which Redfield's
conception of the village culture and community as an
organic whole appears to be centrally prominent. In an
earlier essay on The Little Community (Chapter 1),
Redfield pointed out that when "the isolated primitive
community alone" is studied by anthropologists it
appears to have a recognizable "cultural homogeneity";
but when the peasant community is studied in its
cultural context, then this "context" appears "to
include the elements of the great tradition that are or
have been in interaction with what is local and
immediate."

[7]In The Little Community (1955:113-131), Redfield
acknowledged analyses of rural-urban socio-cultural
structures by Starr, Hanssen and Steward shedding light
on life in peasant communities and "partly urbanized"
rural communities whose "imagined total structure" is
qualitatively different from "the very different kinds
of life and kinds of communities belonging to towns and
cities." Moreover, in Peasant Society and Culture
(1955:45), Redfield contrasted the "primary" and
"secondary" civilizations as being either "indigenous
and self-evolving," or else as being foreign, imported,
and superimposed upon an indigenous primary
civilization, and producing thereby a "hybrid
civilization."

[8]Marriott (1955:181) explained that an "indigenous"
or "primary" civilization develops within a typical
peasant community environment through a progressive
expansion of "the cultural consciousness of persons
within it as they become aware of a greater sphere of
common culture."

[9]Marriott (1955:196) also noticed certain features
in Hindu village festivals which appear only loosely and
vaguely interconnected with the Hindu "Great Tradition,"
and certain other features which entirely lack this
connection. This partial integration of the features
indicates the ongoing process of brahmanization of the
village festivals and their "little tradition" moving
from the partial to the complete "sanskritization" of
their forms as explained by Srinivas (1952:20f.).

[10]Marriott thought that the acculturational
processes of upward "universalization" and downward
"parochialization" could "account for the present
distribution of many religious elements between great
and little communities in India." On the other hand,

Marriott (1955:201f.) also admitted that, since both processes must have already continued for a very long time, it is now "impossible to ascertain with certainty which of the constituent elements of a given traditional religious configuration of the Indian socio-culture" could have been the result of one or the other of the two processes.

[11]S. J. Tambiah (1970:368f.) also found historical inaccuracies in Dumont's and Pocock's resolution of Marriott's problem on the relation of the religion of the typical Hindu village to the "Great Tradition" of Sanskritic Hinduism. Tambiah thought that they had merely substituted a different terminology for Marriott's concepts and theories of "sanskritization," "universalization," and "parochialization" while retaining his notion of "the traditional higher sanskritic civilization" providing India's socio-cultural unity, and of "the lower or popular level of culture and Hinduism." Nevertheless, they understood the stratificational complexity of the socio-culture indicated by "the levels and constituent units of Hinduism" - for example, brahmanic, sectarian, literary, tantrika, popular, and folk Hinduism - which they discussed in their essay on "World Renunciation in Indian Religion" (1960).

[12]Tambiah (1970:369) discussed the relations between the "lower" and the "higher" level religion in different terms. He thought that "homologous structures of ideas and relationships can be discovered" both in popular religious practice and in the religion's "literary disquisitions" although their respective "idioms" are different.

[13]Tambiah (1970:372-373) attempted a more realistic characterization of the Thai religion by rejecting the "two levels" distinctions which are "frequently inapplicable to the anthropologist's field data and experience." For whereas anthropologists usually contrasted professionals representing the higher literary tradition of Hinduism or Buddhism, and locals practicing the lower-level popular forms of the religion, Tambiah emphasized the network of communicational and functional interlinkages reflecting the historic integration of both levels of the religious beliefs and practices of members of a little community. In this light, Tambiah (1970:374f.) concluded, in an argument tantamount to making obsolete the notion of the "historical" and contemporary "levels" in Redfield's socio-cultural paradigm, that the historic or

traditional Buddhism is like Sanskritic Hinduism or
Brāhmanism inasmuch as its explanation "would comprise,
not only the range of religious texts written in the
past, but also the changes in the institutional forms of
Buddhism over the ages." "Contemporary religion"
accordingly, is the ancient religion "as it is practiced
today" including its historical texts in present-day
use, and ancient customs surviving within "the
[presently] ongoing religion."

[14]A. L. Kroeber's "anthropological view" of
cultural-history includes the supposition that change is
an integral feature of cultures. Cultures intersperse
periodic cumulative or climactic peaks of "cultural
florescence" showing successful reconstitutions of
organized "ideas, standards and substyles" with
intervening periods of sterility, decline and dormancy.
Milton Singer expanded upon Kroeber's ideas on the
"periodization" of "growth tendencies" in cultures by
including foreign cultural inflows comprising artistic,
scientific, and other cultural substyles, and even
"total life-styles." These have generated the hybrid
socio-cultural structures - such as the mergence of
folk-communities or peasant-societies with urban
counterparts - with their networks of social and
cultural interconnections and hybrid civilizational
backdrops.

Chapter Two. Great Tradition and Little Tradition
     Buddhism in Śrī Laṅkā

[1]Wherever historical and cultural geographers have
noticed changes in climate and changes in the courses of
major waterways as significant influences upon cultures,
including the "drift" of ideas, cultural-historians have
found evidences of cultural syncretism or the "drift" of
cultures. The diffusions of cultures, and their
regional and local acculturations, are historically
relevant and can be illustrated by the spread of
Sanskritic Hinduism throughout India, and more
specifically, in the spread of the ancient Harappan
culture in North India. In this regard, and despite his
stated lack of interest in the movement of "cultural
complexes in their entirety," William Kirk's article on
"The Role of India in the Diffusion of Early Cultures"
(1975:19-34) is highly informative on cultural-change in
the Buddhist world even while being focussed upon "those
elements [in the Harappan culture] that act as
indicators of the leading margins of innovation waves"
as well as in "the direction in which the tide flows
most strongly."

[2]Milton Singer's interpretation of the socio-cultural setting of "sectarian Hinduism" within the manifold of the brahmanic "Great Tradition" of India sheds light upon the contemporaneous socio-cultural setting of Jainism and Buddhism during their formative periods around the sixth century B.C. Moreover, Singer's explanation of the brahmanic "Great Tradition" integration with the sectarian-Hindu popular religion usefully indicates certain elements of the ancient brahmanical tradition which were carried over into Buddhism and developed within it.

[3]Dumont and Pocock (1959, 1960) also found the theory deficient in regard to that "mainland India" context, particularly in regard to Marriott's understanding of the interrelation of the Sanskritic Hindu "Great Tradition" and the "Little Tradition" of folk-religion in village India. Moreover, Tambiah (1970) endorsed their criticisms in a preface to his own attempts at fitting the concepts and theory of the Redfield-Marriott dichotomy into a positivistic socio-historical account of Buddhism in its South Asian socio-cultural context.

[4]Robert Redfield generally indicated and McKim Marriott specifically illustrated the real conditions of a typical Hindu village culture of Northern India. Redfield contended that "indigenous Great Traditions" develop uniquely through "universalizations" of some folk-culture elements, return into the folk-culture through "parochializations" of certain "Great Tradition" elements, but generally remain in a reciprocal relationship with the "Little Tradition" without ever becoming totally appropriated by or absorbed into it. The criterion behind the selection or non-selection of "Great Tradition" elements is their religious significance or utility. This partial accommodation of the two traditions on the ground of pragmatical relevances indicated by Redfield and developed by Marriott seems to be overlooked in Obeyesekere's criticism of Marriott's views on the institutionalizing of a Great Tradition within a peasant socio-culture.

[5]Marriott's own presentation may have been the source of their misunderstandings of the concepts and their relations, in particular his theory of the development of an indigenous great tradition within a peasant culture through its universalization of pragmatically-relevant components and elements. It should be pointed out, however, that Marriott did not confuse this upward process of universalized local folk-

tradition elements with the downward indigenizing movement of the hybrid "Great Tradition" of Sanskritic Hinduism. Instead, he conjectured on the probability that the indigenous great tradition and the all-India great tradition must have become interconnected quite early in the development of the all-India Hinduism.

[6]If Obeyesekere read de Young correctly, then it must be admitted that de Young misunderstood the connotations of the "socio-cultural levels" which Redfield and Marriott had intended. These scholars indicated that the levels are dynamic developments, and this dynamic feature is apparent when little communities are not studied as primitive isolates but as interlinked systems connected by the networks of services and communications which comprise the socio-cultural interrelations of peasant-communities in village India.

[7]Obeyesekere emphasized that "animism" is not a real feature of peasant cultures as so many of his contemporaries seem to have assumed. Indeed, the notion of a substantively distinguishable "animistic tradition" in the religion of the peasant-folk stems solely from a misinterpretation of Redfield's and Marriott's theory of peasant socio-cultures. For these had admitted that even if the members of primitive communities practice some kind of naive magical-animism, this is not accountable as an integral part of their religion. Furthermore, inasmuch as the socio-culture of any village community is only a less sophisticated form of the larger socio-culture in which it is imbedded, representations of the folk-systems as "primitive" or as "magical-animistic" are misleading as well as inappropriate. Unfortunately, the "animistic myth" is all too frequently presented in socio-anthropological statements on village India and on peasant socio-cultures of South Asia.

[8]M.M.J. Marasinghe's notable study of early Theravāda Buddhist theism in Gods in Early Buddhism (1974) is a valuable counter-argument showing that in the development of the early Buddhist cosmology there was also the development of a complex Buddhist theism replete with an hierarchical pantheon of higher and lower supernatural beings oriented aroung the presidency of the divine Buddha. This served as the Buddhist counterpart of the contemporaneous Brahmanical cosmology and theism in the same period. Hence, although the Nikāya-literature does not appear to portray the supernaturals as deities in the conventional sense of beings who are worshipped and propitiated by the

worshippers, there is only a fine margin between the intellectual disdain toward a theistic interpretation of the Buddha and his court and the popular responsiveness to such an interpretation found in the devotional outlook and practices of the majority of the Buddhist laity and clergy.

[9]In his preface, Marasinghe strongly stressed the importance for historical scholarship on Buddhism of the brahmanic socio-culture behind the development of the distinctive "Buddhist" theism and particularly for recognizing the integral relation of the muted theism of the Buddhist Nikāyas and the explicit theism of popular Buddhism. In this regard, the record of Buddhist development in theism includes not only the textual monuments but also archeological and artistic monuments which visually reflect the cultural fusions - between Brahmanic theism and Buddhist religion - which shaped the character and substance of an early Buddhist theistic system. They also indicate that "Buddhistic" forms of popular theism developed in relation to and contemporaneously with the system of "meditation-deities" represented in the early documents of monastic Buddhism, that is, in the manner illustrated by modern socio-anthropological studies of popular traditional Buddhism in contemporary Buddhist South Asia. In this light, the relative sparse theism presented in the Nikāyas may reflect an early intellectualization of early Buddhism stemming the tide of a popular admixing of Brahmanical, Buddhist, and aboriginal heroes and saints into its theistic pantheon.

[10]The pictorial representations of the Buddhist religion on the stupas and other surviving architectural and artistic monuments of ancient India illustrate the organic integrality of normative and popular Theravāda Buddhist religion in northern India. The exuberantly intricate ornamentational interweavings of aniconic and iconic symbolism, and the pictographic animatistic and heroic narrative in which the grandiosely humanized and divinely apotheosed Buddha and his entourage of disciples are visually represented against the backdrop of a nature mysticism represented by symbolic fauna, flora, and the hybrid human-animal and floral-animal forms all mirror the real complexity of the early Buddhist religion due to the diverse contemporary levels of religious belief and practice among Buddhists in all walks of life and in every stratum of the Buddhist community in North India. They show that no "level" can be totally dissociated from the primary Buddhism of ancient India.

[11]In The Conception of Punishment in Early Indian Literature (1982:153-165), T. P. Day attempted a conceptual integration of the seemingly contradictory fatalistic and retributional theories of human life and misfortunes by comparing Vedic and Dharmasastrika statements. He concluded that the parallel ideas and theories of divine judgement, karmic retribution, fate, demonic interventions, and natural calamities presuppose recognition of diverse causes of human suffering and misfortune and provisions of diverse remedial measures for them.

[12]Michael Ames (1964b:22) pointed out the more prominent non-Theravāda "institutions" of the Sinhalese as being magical-animism, monastic landlordism and state-patronage. The artificiality of this differentiation is apparent, however, in his remark that they are "always closely associated with Buddhism."

[13]T. P. Day's written introduction to "Karma and Moral Causation" (1982:72-73) indicates the development of a normative or "Great Tradition" view of Karma out of the common, everyday usages of the word carrying the sense of self-willed action.

[14]Robert Redfield expressed a hope, in Peasant Society and Culture (1956), that scientists would indicate empirically the "communicational interlinkages" joining the cultures of the "urban sophisticates" and the "village peasants" in the regions of their socio-scientific explorations. He recognized in Marriott's sociological study of the Indian village, Kishan Garhi, a first significant step toward empirically indicating such connections. Milton Singer's lengthy study of Sanskritic Hinduism in metropolitan Madras and its suburbs shows considerable interest in its "Great Tradition/Little Tradition" communicational interlinkages. Redfield might also have recognized Obeyesekere's exposition of the "shared concepts" and "salvation idiom" between the urban and the peasant followers of Sinhalese Buddhism as a further empirical endorsement of his "communicational interlinkage" theory on the conjoining of "Great Tradition" and "Little Tradition" systems in "secondary" cultures and civilizations. Obeyesekere (1963:152 n.20) particularly pointed out that "the idiom of salvation" shared by urban and peasant Buddhists in South Asia "is not the only channel of communication and mutual reference between the two traditions." He noted that "cultural forms like astrology" are "scholastic" in the "Great Tradition" and ritualistic and magical in the "Little

Tradition." Medicine also is philosophical and empirical in the "Great Tradition," "but heavily magical in the Little." Michael Ames recognized also the commonality of "the salvation idiom" but found its meaning and goal to be different in the great tradition of the urban laity, and in the little tradition of the rural peasant-folk. On the other hand, his recognition of the interchangeability of salvific and materialistic functions of the "sacred" and the "profane" rituals performed by members of the higher and lower traditions causes his clear-cut structural and functionalistic distinctions between the great and the little tradition expressions of the Sinhalese religion to break down, particularly on account of their fusion within the complex living organism of the Sinhalese religion.

[15]Ames in the context of Sinhalese religion, like Spiro in the context of Burmese religion, developed the notion of a dualistic "division of labor and . . . allocation of crucial religious roles" among monks and "priests of the lower cults." Obeyesekere had envisaged these in connection with the contradictory "spiritual salvific goals of Theravāda Buddhism" and the "materialistic" goals of "popular religion." Ames, on the other hand, heavily underscored these contrasts by attributing the category of "religion" or "the sacred" to the "salvific goal" functions, and the category of "the profane" or "non-religion" to the materialistically-motivated magic-rituals of the Sinhalese Buddhist population.

[16]Although Ames (1964b:34 & 35) did not critically address Obeyesekere's studies of the Sinhalese religion, he did cite Obeyesekere's 1958 and 1962 works.

[17]Ames (1964b:31) explained that since the "popular" and the "sophisticate" Buddhism are based on two different types of Buddhist "ritual," respectively of "merit-making" rites and "meditation," they are both "sacred" as well as "highly systematized". The real difference between them is societal inasmuch as "merit-making is for the masses and meditating for the few religious sophisticated virtuosos." "Pinkama, or merit-making is the core of folk, popular, or worldly Buddhism."

[18]In the light of this physical organization of the "shrine Buddhism," any empirically and historically sound representation of Sinhalese Buddhism requires a socio-cultural backdrop showing the contemporaneous expression of diverse types and systems of the religion.

This would not be along such lines as Ariyapala (1956) and Wirz (1954) followed denigrating the shrine-Buddhism and the folk-Buddhism of the Sinhalese peasants by seeing them as vulgarizations of an original pure and pristine Buddhism.

[19]Ames' definitional contrasts between Theravāda Buddhist rituals and Sinhalese "magical rituals" are too imprecise for scientific comparison. His insistence that Buddhist ritual is not a "science" (vidyava) - like "the science of spirits" (bhutavidyava) - but is a "faith" (agama) is contentious and not empirically verifiable. It is even doubtful in view of the interchangeability of "magical" and "propitiatory" rituals both of which Ames (1964b.38) recognized as dealing with "polluted (kilutu) entities external to the psyche."

[20]Even before the start of the nineteen-eighties, Milton Singer's dualistic Great Tradition/Little Tradition characterization of Sanskritic Hinduism was being interpretationally applied as in L.A. Corwin's study of small Bengali-town elites in Contributions to Indian Sociology (New Series) (1977).

[21]Evers' perception of the incompleteness of Theravāda Buddhism due to its lack of essential componential appurtenances is similar to Kirsch's representation of it (1977:247) as "abstract Buddhism." However, Kirsch later widened the reference by perceiving "Thai Buddhism" as embracing Theravāda Buddhism in the fullest sense required for a "complete religious system" alongside other contemporary complete religious systems such as "folk-brāhmanism" and "animism."

[22]A. Thomas Kirsch (1977:242 n.4) noted the discussion. Heinz Bechert (1978:197) modified the notion of Theravāda Buddhism as an "incomplete religion" by pointing out that, although in some regions of South Asia, Theravāda Buddhism visibly lacks some of the essential components of a "complete" religion, this "incompleteness" cannot be generalized since religiously complete versions of Theravāda Buddhism have existed and survived, for example, among the Barua Theravāda Buddhists in contemporary Bengal.

[23]In Monks, Priests, and Peasants (1972:99, n.1), Evers cited one of his earlier works (1965), also quoted Yalman (1965:44), and cited Ames (1964b) on the difficulty of speaking of a "dual organization" of the

Sinhalese religion "where the society itself is not so divided." He concluded that it is more appropriate to conceptualize the religion as a unified "symbolic system" having prominent "binary categories."

[24]K.R. Norman (1976:468) rejected Evers' conception of a distinguishable "palace system" in the Sinhalese religion principally because he failed to provide empirical validation for his historical theory that a "palace-cult of the god-king" developed among the Kandyan aristocracy as the distinct political or secular part of a tripartite Buddhist religion which included also the vihara-system of Buddha-worship and the devala-system or shrine-Buddhism comprising the worship of Buddhist and buddhaized Sinhalese deities.

Seneviratne (1977:381-383) did not dispute Evers' "palace-system" religion-theory but only his assumption that such a system actually existed from early times in ancient Ceylon. In this regard, Evers had cited Geiger (1960:176) as his authority for the earliest mention of devales in the Pali literature, and had cited Rahula (1956:43) to support the view that a dual theistic and atheistic Buddhism had coexisted even from the third century B.C. These two authorities also provided the tenuous informational ground for Evers' historical theory of a "court-Buddhism" or "palace-religion" system in ancient Ceylon.

[25]Bechert approached his study of Sinhalese Theravāda Buddhism as an Indologist (Buddhologist) in the University of Gottingen, Germany, but did so from a socio-historical perspective. His indebtedness to the sociologists of religions in South and Southeast Asia during the nineteen-sixties and seventies is manifest by his frequent citations of their works, his using of their information in prefaces to his textual-historiographical studies in Buddhism, and the overall socio-historical orientation of his interpretations and explanations of Theravāda Buddhism's regional historic expressions. In regard to the Redfield-Marriott dichotomy, Bechert acknowledged the interpretive utility of the Great Tradition/Little Tradition concepts particularly for elucidating the contrastive rural and urban contexts of South Asia's traditional religions.

[26]In his discussion of the Great Tradition/Little Tradition dimensions of "popular Buddhism," Bechert adopted Obeyesekere's Redfieldian terminology but not his definition of the Sinhalese religion for reasons which he stated in "Einige Fragen der Religionssoziologie" (1948:266-275), note 1).

[27]Bechert (1970:774) recognized "a typical example of popular Buddhism" in "the little tradition sense" in "the half-magical practices" indicated in Vedeha's thirteenth-century Pali text, the Rasavahīnī.

[28]This syncretic view of religion in Sinhalese Buddhism is supported elsewhere. In Precept and Practice: Traditional Buddhism in the Rural Highlands of Ceylon (1971), Richard Gombrich showed that he had in mind the Buddhism throughout Buddhist South Asia, particularly by his statement that "non-Buddhist intrusions" have had a long history in the Buddhist tradition. In a comment on Gombrich's statement, A. Thomas Kirsch (1977:243, n.10) aptly concluded that "the effort to distinguish between Buddhist and non-Buddhist features [of a religion in Buddhist South Asia] may be fraught with difficulty."

[29]The multiplication of South Asian Theravada Buddhist systems in Bechert's characterization of the religion is not a defect in Bechert's analysis of the total system but was an outcome of the current analytical method of interpretation indicated by Terwiel in his essay on "A Model for the Study of Thai Buddhism" (1975:391-403) which has a "survey" of current sociological literature on the subject as a preface.

[30]In the "survey" on "the literature on the practice of religion in Theravada Buddhist countries," Terwiel (1975:391-392) indicated that his own study of Thai Buddhism would be based on the distinction between the "unsophisticated Buddhism" of the Thais and "the Buddhism of the educated people," and also on his "feeling" that the Thai people continue to be members of one single religion even though Thailand's elites "may well feel that there is a discrepancy between the Great Tradition [Buddhism] and the manifold accretions."

Chapter Three. Burmese Animism and Theravāda Buddhism

[1]Among the few references to Brohm's essay on Burmese religion, Spiro acknowledged it in Burmese Supernaturalism (1967:264) where he interpreted Brohm (1963:165) as arguing that only a "conceptual syncretism" exists between "Buddhism and animism" in Burma, there being no "substantive syncretism" such as King (1964:62) supposed. Unfortunately, Brohm's summary conclusions do not support Spiro's contention.

[2]Brohm's "generalizations" included expositions of the "cyclical" (i.e. calendrical), "maturational,

diurnal, and lunar" manifestations and the "non-cyclical" manifestations of Burmese religious behaviour drawn from analyses of their content previously represented as "whole units" and of the specific attitudes which each of these "units" reflects. He also generalized about "the social structure" in which the indicated behaviour occurs. He also analyzed the structure in terms of its "several special categories-such as monks, nuns, [and] Brahmans," village "leadership roles," corporate and individual ritualistic "interactions with the supernatural," "religious interest groups," etc., and also the behavioural structure including evidences of Burmese religious adaptability to "borrowed elements" diffused from "non-Buddhist" sources and "assimilated into the religious system."

[3]Despite Brohm's perceptive recognition of an animistically-enlivened Burmese Theravāda Buddhism, implications of that perception were not taken up by other members of his scholarly community researching Buddhist South Asian religions.

[4]Spiro (1970:4, n.2) noticed a "self-conscious methodological stance" by "some social scientists" which excluded canonical Buddhism from their considerations. He found this "exclusivistic extreme" in Tambiah's earlier work (1968:43) and compared it with "the other extreme" in the works of "scientists, who, like Max Weber (1958), assume that normative Buddhist doctrine is more or less identical with the beliefs of practicing Buddhists."

[5]Spiro's Freudian exploration of the psycho-dynamics of Buddhist/Supernaturalistic integration in Burmese religion was not easily amenable to historical considerations. Moreover, his distinctions between the three types of "normative Buddhism" appear conceptualistic rather than empirical, and their explanation structural-functionalistic rather than historical. In regard to his interpretations of the normative traditions, Gombrich (1972:491) found "some muddle about the historical sources of the three types." Gombrich also thought that Spiro's presentation on the problem of the historical origins of the three normative types disclosed also a "conceptual muddle" in regard to how each of the three types is "canonical."

[6]Spiro's typical Burmese village of Yeigyi comprised "nuclear" families in one hundred and nineteen houses forming a population of around five-hundred

people living within an area having paddy-fields with
irrigation for wet rice cultivation on three sides and
foothills on the fourth side, three monasteries with a
combined population of "four resident monks and a
somewhat larger number of temporary and transient
novices," and a "socio-cultural matrix of life"
combining "farming and sex, gossip and intrigue, worship
and celebration, pilgrimage and festival."

[7]Although Richard Gombrich (1972:489) disliked
Spiro's habit of referring to the nat-cult as "the nat-
cultus," he expressed "vehement agreement" with most of
what Spiro "says" about "the general relationship with
Buddhism" of the nat-cult. This "agreement" is
problematic, however, since the relationship is a
conceptual one held by the social scientists, not an
empirical duality, in the real religion of Burma's
Buddhist population. Yet Gombrich's approval of the
conceptual dichotomy appears to stem from its harmony
with his own fieldwork in the rural highlands of Ceylon
since Gombrich (1972:489, n.2) stated his own
"qualifications" for reviewing Spiro's work as deriving
from "an acquaintance with Pali Buddhist texts and
detailed first-hand knowledge of Buddhism in central
Ceylon."

[8]Spiro (1967:248-249) noticed these "buddhaizing"
propensities in the Burmans' "witting and unwitting
attempts" at providing "Buddhist sanction" for the
aboriginal "nat-system." But a complete picture would
have included reciprocal tendencies of acculturating
indigenization showing how the originally imported
Theravada Buddhism became popularized through its
accommodation into the Burmese pre-Buddhist, aboriginal
primal-tradition.

[9]The "doctrinal conflict" which Spiro (1967:257-
263) found between the popular notion of Karma and the
"propitiation of nats" in the belief-system of his
monastic informants was more certainly an
"inconsistency" than a "conflict." Similarly, "the
conflict of ethos" which Spiro found between the "set of
values" appertaining to the Burman's "Buddhist" and
"non-Buddhist" systems indicates a contrastive rather
than an oppositional duality.

[10]Spiro (1967:279) concluded that, although "the
nat cultus" is "prohibited" by Buddhist scripture, it
had been "permitted" by the Buddhist leaders as their
concession to "the bacchanalian needs" of the Burmans
and as a recourse for safeguarding the purity of the

pristine Buddhism from the sensuality and superstitions of the aboriginals. Spiro decided, however, that this concession - the <u>nat</u> cultus" - is not <u>religious</u> by reserving the word "religion" solely for Burmese Buddhism and deleting the religion label from Burmese "non-Buddhist" supernaturalistic and animistic beliefs and practices.

Chapter Four. The Transformational Process in Thai Theravāda Buddhism

[1]The discussion of Mus' ideas is richly informed by Frank Reynolds' important and extensive reviews of his complicated and prolix interpretational works on the brahmanical socio-culture in mainland and further India. Reynolds (1981:228) incidentally mentioned "Stanley Tambiah's subsequent discussion" of Mus' interpretational "perspectives and insights"; and in a review of Tambiah's major work on urban Thai Buddhism (1976) through his use of the work of Paul Mus, moved beyond his earlier work on <u>Buddhism and the Spirit Cults in North-East Thailand.</u>"

[2]In the opinion of Reynolds (1981:228f.), Mus' socio-anthropological approach to the brahmanical socio-culture of South Asia developed out of his thesis that Indian religion is not "an essentially Aryan tradition which absorbs a number of indigenous elements," but instead, is "an essentially Aryan tradition that creatively appropriates Aryan and other influences that come [<u>sic</u>] into the area from the West." Reynolds also indicated that Mus defined his approach as "the concern to explore and highlight processes through which the intrinsic potentialities of accepted concepts, practices, and symbols are actualized over the course of time." These "processes" include the "diverse responses" which they evoke.

[3]The intellectualistic or theoretical perspective in Mus' account of the developmental process in religions appears in his "Preface" to <u>Barabadur</u> (1935), but also in later studies in which Reynolds found a "reconstruction of the religious history of South and Southeast Asia." There, Mus worked out how "abstract representations couched in terms of new composite religious ideations brought about by the challenges, enrichments, compromises, and reassertions" of externally impacting socio-cultural influences must have produced "new forms" and "radically new versions" of the historic traditions.

[4]Mus' personalistically-worded sentences are inappropriate for describing changes in the ideological components of the religions of Hindu and Buddhist South Asia. The conceptualistic metaphors to which the personalistic statements are applied are also scientifically problematic because they are confused with the _real_ components and organizations of the religions which developed during many centuries into their present-day forms.

[5]Mus derived his socio-cultural anthropological approach to South and Southeast Asia from the theoretical sociology of Emile Durkheim, Marcel Mauss, and Levi Bruhl. These showed "cultural anthropologists" and other social scientists a way out from their uncritical and often naive dependence upon the current Indological/Buddhological scholarship on religions in South Asia principally by indicating the historiographical viability of ethnographic field-data subjected to a combination of historical and sociological theory and analytical method.

[6]Tambiah's critique of Spiro's psychologistic dualization of the Burmese religion shows that his own interpretive approach was moving away from the current socio-scientific accentuations of the Redfield-Marriott dichotomy.

[7]Although Tambiah professed greater interest in the "tensions" or "parameters" within the Thai religion which "derive primarily from historical Buddhism," his actual interpretations of Thai _supernaturalism_ and Thai _Buddhism_ were unavoidably influenced by the Redfieldian dualities currently used by his scientific contemporaries.

[8]Heinz Bechert had pursued this line of historical inquiry in his major work on Buddhism and politics in South Asia of the post-War II period in _Buddhismus, Staat und Gesellschaft in den Ländern des Theravāda-Buddhismus_ (1966).

[9]Tambiah made the point that sufficient knowledge of the socio-cultural contexts of Theravāda Buddhism in any given region and at any given historical period would provide the background for characterizations of the "parameters" or "underlying set of paradoxes and dialectical tensions" in historical Buddhism which have been the source of the changing "patterns" or temporal crystallizations of the Theravāda tradition in South Asia.

[10]Bechert presented his explorations of the empirical background of the historic relationship of the Buddhist monastic order and national politics in South Asia in Buddhismus, Staat und Gesellschaft (1966) and also in an essay on "Theravāda Buddhism and Mass Politics" in D.E. Smith (ed.), Religion and Political Modernization (1974). The history of the Buddhist ideology of monkhood and its changes between classical and modern times are outlined by Walpola Rahula in The Heritage of the Bhikkhu (1974). Rahula thought that its ideological change "has to be judged either as the bringing into prominence of the concept of anagārika, for example, in the face of new conditions giving it fresh meaning and relevance, or [as] the invention of an entirely new meaning of the concept through the impact of modernity." Obeyesekere's remark on this matter in "Religious Symbolism and Political Change in Ceylon" (1972) is particularly illuminating when read in the light of Bechert's exposition - in "Saṅgha, State, Society, Nation" (1973) - on the transformation of the Buddhist ideal of sainthood, including "the Bodhisattva ideal," in the "post-traditional context" of Buddhist societies in Southeast Asia. The historic influence of this Bodhisattva-ideal on the "political tradition" in Burma is amply discussed by E. Sarkisyanz in Buddhist Backgrounds of the Burmese Revolution (1965:43-48).

[11]Barber and King (1973:125) valued Tambiah's kaleidoscopic model of "the total field of Thai religion" as "the most useful and comprehensive model to date in the analysis of the complex relations existing between Buddhism, Brahmanism, and spirit cults at the village level." They nevertheless doubted that the Baan Phraan Muan area of Northeast Thailand which Tambiah had made the locus of his study of rural Thai religion was authentically representative of the Thai socio-culture since "all [that] he is describing is far nearer in character to what would be found in Laos than what is the norm for Bangkok and the Menam valley."

[12]Terwiel cites: Wales (1931:307-307), Aung (1962), Ames (1963:21-49), Dutt (1966:78), Pfanner (1966:94-95), and Rabibhadana (1969:11).

[13]Terwiel cited: Trager (1960:533-534), Mendelsohn (1963:94-116), Obeyesekere (1963:40), Nash (1966:17-35); Wright (1968:1), and Rajadhon (1968:33).

[14]Cited by Terwiel were: Velder (1936:92), R. Le May (1954:163), Amyot (1965:153-154), Ebihara (1966:189-191), and Bunnag (1973:18-23).

[15]Spiro (1966:93-94); (1967:265-271)

[16]Terwiel cited: Credner (1935:342-343), Kingshill (1960:92), Textor (1960:8-12), Kirsch (1967), and Attagora (1968).

[17]This compartmentalization can be found in the study of rural Thai religion by S.J. Tambiah (1970:1-5).

[18]Terwiel indicated that his own research on Thai religion was "inspired by the discrepancies and opposing views" in current sociological literature on the structure of Theravada Buddhism. He hoped that his own researches would enable him "to decide whether the syncretists or those favoring a compartmentalization of religious belief had the more suitable approach." He indicated his methodological approach as primary fieldwork using "in-depth interviews" combined with participant-observation of the religion as a monastery-dwelling "fully ordained member of the Saṅgha" followed by "half of the year lived as a layman on a farm" where he could silently observe the daily practices and attitudes behind the religious beliefs and behaviour of the Thai country-folk.

[19]Terwiel (1975:393) found both the conceptual categories currently used by scientists for distinguishing "Buddhist" from "non-Buddhist" practices, and their questions regarding the conformity or non-conformity of those practices with "canonical orthodoxy," highly problematic for their local Buddhist informants.

[20]These contrasts are summarily represented in Table III of Terwiel's essay (1975:403).

[21]Kirsch (1977:242) cited K. Landon (1939) and R. Le May (1926) in reference to "the historical approach." These early references suggest that Kirsch thought the historical approach to be outdated and "the structural-functional approach" as being "favored by most contemporary anthropologists and other social scientists interested in Theravāda Buddhism."

[22]Kirsch thought that recognizing "Buddhism" and also "Buddhist society" as "single enduring entities that can be abstracted from the flux of particular social life" can be useful especially for ascertaining the interrelations of complex religious systems and societies influenced by Theravāda Buddhism. However, "Buddhism" and "Buddhist societies" are "variables"

subject to events, circumstances, and exterior forces
impacting upon them and effecting changes within them.

[23]Kirsch may have presented those nine forms as
indicating <u>nominal</u> rather than <u>historical</u> differences
since the "sophisticated Buddhism," "formal Buddhism,"
"abstract Buddhism," and "doctrinal Buddhism" appear to
reflect Weberian "ideal types" rather than distinctive
<u>historic</u> traditions.

Bibliography of Citations

Ames, Michael M. "Buddha and the Dancing Goblins: A Theory of Magic and Religion." American Anthropologist 66, No.1 [1964].

_____. "Magical Animism and Buddhism: A Structural Analysis of the Sinhalese Religious System." Journal of Asian Studies XXIII, No. 2 [1964b].

_____. "Ritual Prestations and the Structure of the Sinhalese Pantheon." Nash, Manning (ed.). Anthropological Studies in Theravada Buddhism. Cultural Report Series No.13. New Haven, Connecticut: Yale University Southeast Asia Studies [1966].

Amyot, J. Changing Patterns of Social Structure in Thailand 1851-1965. Delhi: Unesco Research Centre [1965].

Ashby, Philip H. History and Future of Religious Thought: Christianity, Hinduism, Buddhism, Jainism. New Jersey: Prentice-Hall [1963].

Attagara, K. The Folk Religion of Non Nai, A Hamlet in Central Thailand. Bangkok: Kurusapha Press [1968].

Aung, Maung Htin. Folk Elements in Burmese Buddhism. London: Oxford University Press [1962].

Barber, Martin & Victor T. King. Rev. of Buddhism and the Spirit Cults in North-east Thailand by S.J. Tambiah. Modern Asian Studies, Vol.7, Pt.1, 1973 pp.121-124.

Bechert, Heinz. Buddhismus, Staat und Gesellschaft in den Ländern des Theravāda-Buddhismus. Frankfurt: Schriften des Instituts für Asienkunde in Hamburg [1966].

_____. "Einige Fragen der Religionssoziologie und Structur des suedasiatischen Buddhismus."

International Yearbook for the Sociology of
Religion 4, 1968, pp. 251-253.

_____. "Theravāda Buddhist Sangha." Some
General Observations on Historical and Political
Factors in its Development." _Journal of Asian_
Studies XXIX, No.4, 1970, 761-777.

_____. "Sangha, State, Society, "Nation":
Persistence of Traditions in "Post Traditional"
Buddhist Societies." _Daedalus_, Vol.102, 1973,
pp.85-96.

_____. "Contradictions in Sinhalese
Buddhism." Bardwell L. Smith (ed.). _Tradition and_
Change in Theravāda Buddhism: Essays on Ceylon and
Thailand in the 19th and 20th Centuries. Leiden:
E.J. Brill [1973]. Rpt. Bardwell L. Smith (ed.).
Religion and Legitimation of Power in Srī Laṅka.
Chambersburg, PA.: Anima Books [1978].

Brohm, John. "Buddhism and Animism in a Burmese
Village." _Journal of Asian Studies_ XXV, No.2,
1963, pp.155-167.

Bunnag, J. _Buddhist Monk, Buddhist Layman: A Study of_
Urban Monastic Organization in Central Thailand.
Cambridge, England: Cambridge University Press
[1973].

Coedes, G. _The Making of South East Asia_. Trans. H.M.
Wright. Berkeley, Calif.: University of
California Press [1966].

_____. _The Indianized States of Southeast_
Asia. Honolulu: East-West Center Press [1968].

Cohen, I. Bernard. _Revolution in Science_. Cambridge,
Mass.: Harvard University Press [1984].

Corwin, Lauren Anita. "Great Tradition, Little
Tradition: the cultural traditions of a Bengal
town." _Contributions to Indian Sociology (NS)_,

Vol.11, No.1, 1977, pp. 21-44.

Credner W. Siam, das Land der Thai. Stuttgard: Engelhorns Nacht [1935].

Day, Terence P. The Conception of Punishment in Early Indian Literature. Waterloo, Ontario: Wilfrid Laurier University Press [1982].

Dumont, Louis. "World Renunciation in Indian Religion." Contributions to Indian Sociology IV. Paris & The Hague: Mouton & Co. [1960].

Dumont, Louis & D.F. Pocock (eds.). Contributions to Indian Sociology I [1957], III [1959], IV [1960]. Paris & The Hague: Mouton & Co.

Durkheim, Emile. De la division du travail social. [1893]. Trans. George Simpson. The Division of Labor in Society. Glencoe, Ill.: The Free Press [1947].

Dutt, Sukumar. The Buddha and Five After-Centuries. London: Luzac [1957].

_____. Buddhist Monks and Monasteries of India. London: George Allen and Unwin [1962].

_____. Buddhism in East Asia. New Delhi: Indian Council for Cultural Relations [1966].

Drekmeier, Charles. Kingship in Early India. Stanford, Calif.: Stanford University Press [1962].

Ebihara, M. "Interrelations between Buddhism and Social Systems in Cambodian Peasant Culture." Conference on Theravada Buddhism. Yale University South East Asian Studies 13, 1966, pp.189-191.

Embree, John F. The Japanese Nation: A Social Survey. NY: Farrar & Rinehart [1945].

Evers, Hans-Deiter. "Buddha and the Seven Gods. The Dual Organization of a Temple in Central Ceylon." Journal of Asian Studies XXVII, No.2, 1968, pp.541-550.

210

_____. Monks, Priests and Peasants. A Study
of Buddhism and Social Structure in Central Ceylon.
Monographs in Social Anthropology and Theoretical
Studies in Honor of Nels Anderson. Publication I.
Leiden: E.J. Brill [1972].

Geiger, Wilhelm. Pali Literature and Language.
Calcutta: University of Calcutta Press [1953].

_____. Culture of Ceylon in Medieval Times.
Ed. Heinz Bechert. Wiesbaden: Otto Harrassowitz
[1960].

Gombrich, Richard. Precept and Practice: Traditional
Buddhism in the Rural Highlands of Ceylon. Oxford:
Clarendon Press [1971].

_____. "Buddhism and Society." Review of
Burmese Supernaturalism by Melford E. Spiro.
Review of Buddhism and Society: a Great Tradition
and its Burmese Vicissitudes by Melford E. Spiro.
Modern Asian Studies Vol.6, No.4, 1972, pp.483-494.

_____. "Knowledge of the Unknowable." Review
of The Buddhist Saints of the Forest and the Cult
of Amulets by S.J. Tambiah. Times Literary
Supplement, March 29, 1985, pp.359-360.

Government of India. Census of India, 1901. Vol.XII,
Part 1, (Burma Report). Rangoon: Government Press
[1902].

Government of India. Census of India, 1911. Vol.IX,
Part 1, (Burma Report). Rangoon: Government Press
[1912].

Harper, Edward B. (ed.). Aspects of Religion in South
Asia. Journal of Asian Studies XXIII, No.2, June,
1964.

Kaufman, N.K. Bangkhaud, A Community Study in Thailand.
NY: J.J. Augustine. First edition [1960]; second
edition [1977].

King, Victor & Martin Barber. Review of <u>Buddhism and the Spirit Cults in North-east Thailand</u> by S.J. Tambiah. <u>Modern Asian Studies</u>, Vol.7, Pt.1, 1973, pp.121-124.

Kingshill, K. <u>Ku Daeng - The Red Tomb. A Village Study in Northern Thailand</u>. Chiangmai: The Prince Royal's College [1960].

Kirk, William. "The Role of India in the Diffusion of Early Cultures." <u>The Geographical Journal</u>, Vol.141, Part 1, March 1975, pp.19-33.

Kirsch, A. Thomas. "Phu Thai Religion Syncretism, A Case Study of Thai Religion and Society." Ph.D. dissertation. Cambridge, Mass.: Harvard University Press [1967].

_____. "Complexity in the Thai Religious System: An Interpretation." <u>Journal of Asian Studies</u> XXXVI, No.2, 1977, pp.241-266.

Kosambi, Damodar Dharmanand. <u>An Introduction to the Study of Indian History</u>. Bombay: Popular Book Depot [1956].

_____. <u>Ancient India: A History of its Culture and Civilization</u>. New York & Cleveland: The World Publishing Co. Meridian Books [1962]; NY: Pantheon Books [1966].

Kroeber, Alfred L. "Configurations of Culture Growth." In Theodore K Kroeber (ed.). <u>An Anthropologist Looks at History</u>. Berkeley & Los Angeles: University of California Press [1963].

_____. "Periodization." In Theodore K. Kroeber (ed.). <u>An Anthropologist Looks at History</u>. Berkeley & Los Angeles: University of California Press [1963].

Kuhn, Thomas S. <u>The Structure of Scientific Revolutions</u>. Chicago: University of Chicago Press

[1962, 1970].

_____. "Second Thoughts on Paradigms." In Frederick Suppe (ed.). The Structure of Scientific Theories. Second edn. Urbana, Ill.: University of Illinois Press [1977].

Lehman, F.K. Review of Buddhism and the Spirit Cults in North-east Thailand by S.J. Tambiah. Journal of Asian Studies XXXI, 1971, pp.724-728.

Ling, Trevor. The Buddha: Buddhist Civilization in India and Ceylon. London: Temple Smith [1973]. NY: Scribner [1973].

Luce, Gordon H. Old Burma - Early Pagan. Louist Valley, NY: J.J. Augustin, Vol.I [1969].

Malinowski, B. Magic, Science and Religion and other Essays. Boston: Beacon Press [1948]; NY: Doubleday [1954].

Marasinghe, M.M.J., Gods in Early Buddhism. A Study in Their Social and Mythological Milieu as depicted in the Nikayas of the Pali Canon. Colombo, Ceylon: University of Sri Lanka Press [1974].

Marriott, McKim. "Little Communities in an Indigenous Civilization." In Village India. Studies in the Little Community by McKim Marriott (ed.). Chicago: University of Chicago Press [1955].

May, R. Le. An Asian Arcady: The Land and Peoples of Northern Siam. Cambridge, W. Heffer [1926].

_____. The Culture of South-East Asia: The Heritage of India. London: George Allen and Unwin [1954].

Mendelson, E. Michael. "The Uses of Religious Scepticism in Modern Burma." Diogenes 41, 1963, pp.94-116.

_____. Ed. John P. Ferguson. Sangha and State in Burma: A Study of Monastic Sectarianism and Leadership. NY: Cornell University Press, 1975.

Mus, Paul. "Cultes indiens et indigenèse au Champa: L'Inde vue de L'Est." Bulletin de L'Ecole Francoise Extreme Orient 33, 1933, pp.367-410. English trans. India seen from the East. Clayton, Victoria: Monash University Centre for Southeast Asian Studies [1975].

_____. Barabadur. Hanoi: Impr. d'Extreme-Orient [1935].

_____. "Thousand-Armed Kannon: A Mystery or a Problem." Journal of Indian and Buddhist Studies, Tokyo, 1964, pp.1-33.

Nash, J.C. "Living with Nats: An Analysis of Animism in Burman Village Social Relations." Conference on Theravada Buddhism. Yale University Southeast Asian Studies 13, 1966, pp.117-135.

Nash, Manning (ed.). Anthropological Studies in Theravāda Buddhism. Cultural Report Series No.13. Yale University Southeast Asian Studies [1966].

Norman, K.R. "Buddhist Studies." Review of Monks, Priests and Peasants by Hans-Dieter Evers. Journal of Modern Asian Studies Vol.10, 1976, pp.466-469.

Obeyesekere, Gananath. "The Structure of Sinhalese Ritual." Ceylon Journal of Historical and Social Studies I, 1958, pp.192-202.

_____. "The Sinhalese Pantheon and its Extension." In Manning Nash (ed.). Proceedings of the Chicago Conference on Theravāda Buddhism. Chicago: University of Chicago Press [1962].

_____. "The Great Tradition and the Little in the Perspective of Sinhalese Buddhism." Journal of Asian Studies XXII, No.2, 1963, pp.139-153.

_____. "The Buddhist Pantheon in Ceylon and
its Extensions." In Manning Nash (ed.).
Anthropological Studies in Theravāda Buddhism.
Cultural Report Series No.13. Yale University
Southeast Asian Studies [1966].

_____. "Religious Symbolism and Political
Change in Ceylon." In Bardwell L. Smith (ed.).
The Two Wheels of Dhamma. Chambersburg, Pa.:
American Academy of Religion [1972].

Oldenberg, Herman. Buddha: His Life, His Order, His
Doctrine. Varanasi, India: Indological Book House
[1971].

Papineau, David. "Giant Steps toward Reality." The
Times Literary Supplement, No.4302, Sept. 13,
1985.

Pfanner, D.E. "The Buddhist Monk in Rural Burmese
Society." Conference on Theravada Buddhism. Yale
University Southeast Asian Studies 13, 1966.

Prebish, Charles S. "Buddhist Studies American Style:
A Shot in the Dark." Religious Studies Review
Vol.9, No.4, Oct. 1983, pp.323-330.

Rabibhadana, A. The Organization of Thai Society in the
Early Bangkok Period, 1782-1873. Cornell
University Press [1969].

Raghavan, V. "Adult Education in Ancient India."
Madras, India: Madras Library Association Memoirs,
1944.

_____. "Variety and Integration in the
Pattern of Indian Culture." Far Eastern Quarterly
15, No.3, August 1956, pp. 497-505.

Rahula, Walpola. History of Buddhism in Ceylon, The
Anurādhapura Period 3rd Century B.C. - 10th Century
A.D. Colombo: M.D. Gunasena [1956, 1966].

_____. The Heritage of the Bhikkhu. NY: Grove Press Inc. [1974].

Rajadhon, Anuman. Essays on Thai Folklore. Bangkok: The Social Science Association Press of Thailand [1968].

Redfield, Robert. "The Folk Society." The American Journal of Sociology LII, No.4, January, 1947, pp. 293-308.

_____. The Primitive World and Its Trans-formations. Ithaca, NY: Cornell University Press [1953].

_____. Peasant Society and Culture. Chicago: University of Chicago Press [1956].

Redfield, Robert & Milton Singer. Comparison of Cultures: The Indian Village. Chicago: Department of Anthropology/University of Chicago Press [1954].

_____. "The Cultural Role of Cities." In Economic Development and Cultural Change 3, No.1, 1954, pp.53-73. Reprint in M.P. Redfield (ed.) Human Nature and the Study of Society. Chicago: University of Chicago Press [1956].

Reynolds, Frank. "From Philology to Anthropology: A Bibliographic Essay on Works Related to Early Theravāda and Sinhalese Buddhism." In Bardwell L. Smith (ed.). The Two Wheels of Dhamma. Essays on the Theravāda Tradition in India and Ceylon. AAR Studies on Religion No.3. Chambersburg, Pa.: American Academy of Religion [1972].

_____. "Totalities, Dialectics, and Trans-formations." Review of World Conqueror and World Renouncer. A Study of Buddhism and Polity in Thailand against a Historical Background by S.J. Tambiah. History of Religions Vol.18, No.1, 1978,

216

pp.258-268.

_____. "Toward a History of Religions in
South and Southeast Asia: Some Reflections on the
Work of Paul Mus." Religious Studies Review,
Vol.7, No.3, July 1981, pp.288-293.

Ryan, Bryce. Sinhalese Village. Miami: University of
Miami Press [1958].

Sarkizyanz, E. Buddhist Backgrounds of the Burmese
Revolution. The Hague: Martinus Nijhoff [1965].

Scott, Sir James George. Burma: A Handbook of
Practical Information. Third edition. London:
Alexander Moring [1921].

Seneviratne, H.L. Review of Monks, Priests and
Peasants: A Study of Buddhism and Social Structure
in Central Ceylon by Hans-Dieter Evers. Journal of
Asian Studies XXXVI, No.2, 1977, pp.381-382.

Schiffer, Michael B. "Methodological Issues in Ethno-
archeology." In R. Gould (ed.). Explorations in
Ethnoarcheology. Albuquerque: University of New
Mexico Press [1978].

Singer, Milton. "Text and Context in the Study of
Contemporary Hinduism." Brahmavidya,
Commemoration Number. Madras: The Adyār Library
and Research Center, 1961. Also in When a Great
Tradition Modernizes. An Anthropological Approach
to Indian Civilization. NY: Praeger Publishers
[1972].

_____. When a Great Tradition Modernizes. An
Anthropological Approach to Indian Civilization.
NY: Praeger Publishers [1972].

Smith, Bardwell L. (ed.). The Two Wheels of Dhamma.
Essays on the Theravāda Tradition in India and
Ceylon. AAR Studies in Religion No.3.
Chambersburg, Pa.: American Academy of Religion

[1972].

_____. "Sinhalese Buddhism and the Dilemmas of Reinterpretation." Contributions to Asian Studies, Vol.3. Leiden: E.J. Brill, 1973.

Smith, Donald Eugene. Religion and Politics in Burma. Princeton, N.J.: Princeton University Press [1965].

_____. South Asian Politics and Religion. Princeton, N.J.: Princeton University Press [1966].

Spiro, Melford E. Burmese Supernaturalism. N.J.: Prentice-Hall, Inc. [1967].

_____. Buddhism and Society: A Great Tradition and its Burmese Vicissitudes. NY: Harper & Row [1970].

Srinivas, M.N. "The Social Structure of a Mysore Village." Bombay: Economic Weekly 3, 1951, pp.105-106.

_____. Religion and Society among the Coorgs of South India. Oxford: The Clarendon Press [1952].

Staal, J.F. "Sanskrit and Sanskritization." Journal of the Asiatic Society 22, No.3, May 1963, pp. 261-275.

Tambiah, Stanley J. "The Ideology of Merit and the Social Correlates of Buddhism in a Thai Village." In E.R. Leach (ed.). Dialectic in Practical Religion. Cambridge, England: The University Press, [1968].

_____. Buddhism and the Spirit Cults in North-east Thailand. London: Cambridge University Press, [1970].

_____. "The Persistence and Transformation of

218

Tradition in Southeast Asia with special Reference
to Thailand." Daedalus Vol.102, 1973, pp. 55-84.

_____. World Conqueror and World Renouncer.
A Study of Buddhism and Polity in Thailand against
a Historical Background. Cambridge Studies in
Social Anthropology 15. London: Cambridge
University Press [1976].

_____. The Buddhist Saints of the Forest and
the Cult of Amulets: A Study in charisma,
hagiography, sectarianism, and millennial Buddhism.
London: Cambridge University Press [1984].

Temple, R.C. The Thirty-Seven Nats. London: W. Griggs
[1906].

Terwiel, B.J. "A Model for the Study of Thai Buddhism."
Journal of Asian Studies XXXV, 1975, pp.391-403.

Textor, R.B. "An Inventory of Non-Buddhist Supernatural
Objects in a Central Thai Village." Cornell
University Ph.D. dissertation, 1960.

Trager, F.N. "Reflections on Buddhism and the Social
Order in Southern Asia." Burma Research Society
Fiftieth Anniversary Publications I, 1960.

Velder, C. "Chao Luang Muak Kham." Journal of the Siam
Society LI, No.1, 1963.

Wales, H.G.Q. Siamese State Ceremonies: Their History
and Function. London: Bernard Quaritch [1931].

Weber, Max. The Religion of India; The Sociology of
Hinduism and Buddhism. Trans. Hans H. Gerth and
Don Martindale. NY: The Free Press; London:
Collier-Macmillan Ltd. [1958].

Wheeler, Sir Mortimer. Early India and Pakistan: to
Ashoka. London: Thames & Hudson: NY: Praeger
Publishing [1959].

_____. The Indus Civilization. Supplementary
volume to the Cambridge History of India, 3rd edn.

London: Cambridge University Press [1968].

Wirz Paul. Exorcism and the Art of Healing in Ceylon.
    Leiden: E.J. Brill [1954].

Wright, M.A. "Some Observations on Thai Animism."
    Practical Anthropology, 1968.

Yalman, Nur. "Dual Organization in Central Ceylon or
    The Goddess on the Tree-top." Journal of Asian
    Studies XXIV, 1965, pp.441-457.

Young, J.E. de Village Life in Modern Thailand.
Berkeley,
    Calif.: University of California Press [1955].

Index of Scholars

STUDIES IN ASIAN THOUGHT AND RELIGION